Practical Exercises for Technical Writing

Writing Remedies

Practical
Exercises for
Technical
Writing

By Edmond H. Weiss

ORYX PRESS
1990

The rare Arabian Oryx is believed to have inspired the myth of the unicorn. This desert antelope became virtually extinct in the early 1960s. At that time several groups of international conservationists arranged to have 9 animals sent to the Phoenix Zoo to be the nucleus of a captive breeding herd. Today the Oryx population is nearly 800, and over 400 have been returned to reserves in the Middle East.

Copyright © 1990 by

The Oryx Press

4041 North Central at Indian School Road

Phoenix, Arizona 85012

Published simultaneously in Canada

Printed and Bound in the United States of America

Library of Conress Cataloging-in-Publication Data

Weiss, Edmond H.
    100 writing remedies : practical exercises for technical writing /
by Edmond H. Weiss.
        p. cm.
    Includes bibliographical references (p.   ).
    ISBN 0-89774-638-4 (alk. paper)
        1. English language--Rhetoric--Problems, exercisies, etc.
2.English language--Grammer--1950- --Problems, excersises, etc.
3. Technical writing--Problems, excersises, etc. 4. Business
writing--Problems, excersises, etc. I. Title. II. Title: One hundred
writing remedies.
PE1413.W515 1990   90-7047
808'.0666--dc20   CIP

For my son, Ryan

CONTENTS

INTRODUCTION

Good Writing Is Rewriting

No one can write or dictate a first draft that is good enough to be a last draft. No one.

Effective writers know that no matter how good they are, their first draft is filled with bugs. Furthermore, they know that the best way to write is to push out the first few drafts quickly, allowing ample time to edit and revise.

Even though a good writer's first draft may be somewhat better than a bad writer's, **neither is fit to read.** People who send or publish their first drafts (this includes the new plague of un-proofread electronic mail) are harming their readers and themselves.

A Good Style Is Invisible

100 Writing Remedies: Practical Exercises for Technical Writing is based on the premise that good writers do everything they can to reduce the burden on their readers. Anything that makes a reader struggle or reread is suspect. In this view, a good style is **invisible:** Readers understand the message, without noticing the style.

Bad writers err in two directions. First, they make careless or ignorant mistakes—everything from misspellings to faulty grammar. Second, they show off and overburden their sentences—with pretentious vocabulary and marathon sentences. In short, bad writers make their style **visible.**

REMEMBER: The more time you spend editing and revising your writing, the more effective you will be in your profession. At first, editing may seem like a waste of time. Later, though, you'll see remarkable benefits in your career and in your relationships at work.

Hardly anyone will say that your writing has improved. Rather, they'll remark on how much smarter you seem lately.

How to Use This Book

100 Writing Remedies addresses the flaws I find most often in the first drafts of business and technical professionals--engineers, programmers, managers. Most people find 80% or 90% of their own problems presented here.

The problems in these sentences are called *bugs*. Although this book cautions writers against the careless overuse of computer jargon, still, the term bug is the most precise name that comes to mind. Like the bugs in computer programs, the problems in these sentences creep in unnoticed, the result of haste, laziness, carelessness, sometimes ignorance. And, as is true of the bugs in programs, there is more than one way to get rid of them. Editors (like programmers) may do anything to eliminate a bug—except add a new bug.

The material in this book is in eight parts, or eight "families of bugs." Each part includes

- a set of problem sentences containing the bugs
- a set of remedies (solutions for the problem sentences)
- a brief lesson on each bug, with additional examples

To use this book, read each problem sentence and look for its bug. When you think you've found it, revise the sentence and compare your answer with the corresponding remedy. If you missed the bug— or if you want more information—read the appropriate text.

Sometimes this process is harder than it sounds. Unlike arithmetic problems, problem sentences frequently contain more than one bug and can always have more than one solution. Often, you'll be convinced that your remedy is better than the one in the book. And you might even be right.

The goal is for us to agree on the **main problem** in the sentence, the important bug. When you revise it, do anything you like—so long as you don't add a new bug. An axiom of editing is that although there is more than one correct way to write a sentence, there are still many bad, incorrect ways. Contrary to what many believe, editing is NOT just a matter of personal preference.

Whose Rules?

Only 27 of the 100 problems listed here are truly errors—forbidden by the textbooks. Most of the bugs are matters of clarity and "correct style." For example, splicing two sentences with a comma is an error (Bug # 83), but using commas to do two conflicting jobs in the same sentence is weak style (Bug # 84). Writing "the criteria is..." is poor grammar (Bug # 79), but using a phrase such as "the decision criteria model selection option" is terrible style (Bug # 46).

But, you say, isn't that just one person's opinion? Isn't style something that belongs to the individual? Like a toothbrush? Yes and No.

Although there are several acceptable ways to write, there are many more unacceptable ways. All the advice in this book, whether or not you agree with it, will **in fact** improve your writing and add to your professional effectiveness. The idea is not to change your style into mine. Rather, the goal is to increase the chances that your messages will get through—clear, clean, with power and results.

Good Writing Is Conservative

The most dangerous notion being taught these days is that any widespread practice of writing or speech will inevitably become acceptable. This mistaken notion allows writers to conclude that, since many of the bugs described here occur regularly in the writing of educated people, there is no cause for criticizing them. If everyone starts sentences with *due to*, how can it be wrong? If everyone misspells *supersede* as *supercede*, won't the dictionary eventually allow it?

The only reasonable position is that, even though language is always changing, not all changes are good for the language. English is hurt when it loses the distinction between *imply* and *infer*, just as it was hurt when it lost the distinction between *you* and *thou*.

In contrast, some changes in tradition are helpful. A more liberal use of dashes and "bullets" has made management communication easier to follow. And permitting sentences to begin with a numeral (1990 *will be a slow year*) is far better than asking writers to spell out the word *nineteen*.

Writing must never be as volatile as speech—because the function of writing is to permit communication across time and space. Most educated adults can understand English written 400 years ago (the King James version of the Bible). Most Americans can read books written by British authors of three centuries. Americans, Jamaicans, and Australians have considerable difficulty with each other's speech, but almost no problem with each other's writing.

Perhaps most important for the readers of this book, conservative style is the style preferred by most of the people who evaluate our work and award promotions. The irony is that even when our bosses are guilty of most of the infractions in *100 Writing Remedies,* they still want the rest of us to write according to the principles advocated here.

If you dispute something I have recommended, pursue the problem. (The authorities for my opinions are discussed in Appendix B.) If you believe my advice is dated, unwarranted, then form your own conclusions. And, if you're especially eager to debate a point, please write to me in care of Oryx Press.

WORDS,
In General

WORD PROBLEMS

The sentences below need editing. Each has one or more word problems. Look for

- misused and inappropriate terms
- three or four words where one will do
- misplaced words
- overblown, show-off vocabulary
- any other unfortunate, imprecise, or distracting word choice

1. I want to be appraised continuously of your progress.

_____

(Remedy: Page 9)

2. The group was comprised of a manager and five programmers.

_____

(Remedy: Page 9)

3. All employees seek a maximization of their compensation situation.

_____

(Remedy: Page 9)

4. The task of the program troubleshooter is to remediate the mistakes made by the junior programmer.

_____

(Remedy: Page 9)

5. The report was delayed by the courier shortage situation.

_____

(Remedy: Page 9)

6. The consensus of opinion is that the job will not be entirely finished until October.

_____

(Remedy: Page 9)

7. Their CRT was oval in shape.

_____

(Remedy: Page 9)

8. It takes a longer period of time to update these files than to create them in the first place.

_____

(Remedy: Page 9)

9. So as to be better able to explain the reason for this proposal, we must first explain our previous activities relative to the inventory control problem.

_____

_____

(Remedy: Page 10)

10. As the update had not been completed, we delayed the quarterly report.

_____

(Remedy: Page 10)

11. Due to our truck drivers' strike, we do not know when your system will be delivered.

_____

(Remedy: Page 10)

12. They had complaints with regard to the turnaround time.

_____

(Remedy: Page 10)

13. The company utilizes a dynamic programming model for its market forecast.

_____

(Remedy: Page 10)

14. At that point in time we were utilizing COBOL for the payroll program.

_____

(Remedy: Page 10)

15. The system has a text justification capability.

_____

(Remedy: Page 10)

16. Before we can turn the system over to the client, it is a requirement that we have complete

    documentation.

_____

_____

(Remedy: Page 10)

17. There is a possibility that they will beat us to publication.

_____

(Remedy: Page 10)

18. In order to help them with their writing, we built style-checking software into the word processor.

_____

(Remedy: Page 11)

19. In consideration of these objections, we are opening the purchase to competitive bidding.

_____

(Remedy: Page 11)

20. Serious mistakes can be prevented by means of the use of effective training.

_____

(Remedy: Page 11)

21. They rotated the passwords for the purpose of having better security.

_____

(Remedy: Page 11)

22. In the event a real fire is encountered, the Fire Department will direct the evacuation of the building.

_____

(Remedy: Page 11)

23. Notice the cost advantage which can be derived from using a data base management system.

_____

(Remedy: Page 11)

24. The amount of administrative records on hand is out of proportion to the amount of program records on hand.

_____

_____

(Remedy: Page 11)

25. All of the necessary decisions were not included in the functional specification.

_____

(Remedy: Page 11)

26. He found six good prospects at the convention, which was better than usual.

_____

(Remedy: Page 11)

27. Programmers who talk about the good old days constantly bore the younger staff members.

_____

(Remedy: Page 12)

28. Copies of the financial statement may only be given to members of the Finance Committee.

_____

(Remedy: Page 12)

29. The new system will be totally dedicated to issuing benefit checks.

_____

(Remedy: Page 12)

30. Their final offer was different than their first.

_____

(Remedy: Page 12)

31. The boss told Jones he had problems.

_____

(Remedy: Page 12)

32. No one believes the management will forget its promises.

_____

(Remedy: Page 12)

WORD REMEDIES

1. I want to be apprised continually of your progress.

     See Bug #1: Confused Pairs (Page 13)

2. The group comprised a manager and five programmers.

     OR

The group was composed of a manager and five programmers.

     See Bug #2: Misused Terms (Page 14)

3. All employees want as much pay as they can get.

     See Bug #3: Overblown Nouns (Page 15)

4. The task of the program troubleshooter is to remedy the mistakes made by the junior programmers.

     See Bug #4: Counterfeit Coins (Page 16)

5. The report was delayed by a lack of couriers.

     See Bug #5: Surplus Nouns (Page 17)

6. The consensus is that the job will not be finished until October.

     See Bug #6: Double-Talk (Page 18)

7. Their CRT was oval.

     See Bug #7: Space-Wasters (Page 19)

8. It takes longer to update these files than to create them.

     See Bug #8: Time-Wasters (Page 20)

9. First, to better understand the reason for this proposal, let us review what we have already done about inventory control.

See Bug #9: Throat-Clearers   (Page 21)

10. Because the update had not been completed, we delayed the quarterly report.

See Bug #10: *Because*-Phobia (Page 22)

11. Because of our truck drivers' strike, we do not know when your system will be delivered.

See Bug #11: *Due to* (Page 23)

12. They had complained about the turnaround time.

See Bug #12: *About*-Phobia (Page 24)

13. The company uses a dynamic programming model for its market forecast.

See Bug #13: *Use*-Phobia (Page 25)

14. Then, we were using COBOL for the payroll program.

See Bug #14: *Now/Then*-Phobia (Page 26)

15. The system can justify text.

See Bug #15: *Can*-Phobia (Page 27)

16. Before we can turn the system over to the client, we must have complete documentation.

See Bug #16: *Must*-Phobia (Page 28)

17. They might beat us to publication.

See Bug #17: *May/Might*-Phobia (Page 29)

18. To help them with their writing, we built style-checking software into the word processor.

    See Bug #18: *To*-Phobia (Page 30)

19. So, we are opening the purchase to competitive bidding.

    See Bug #19: *So*-Phobia (Page 31)

20. Serious mistakes can be prevented by effective training.

    See Bug #20: *By/With*-Phobia (Page 32)

21. They rotated the passwords for better security.

    See Bug #21: *For*-Phobia (Page 33)

22. If there is a real fire, the Fire Department will direct the evacuation of the building.

    See Bug #22: *If*-Phobia (Page 34)

23. Notice the cost advantage of a database management system.

    See Bug #23: *Of*-Phobia (Page 35)

24. The number of administrative records on hand is out of proportion to the number of program records on hand.

    See Bug #24: Digital/Analog (Page 36)

25. Not all of the necessary decisions were included in the functional specification.

    See Bug #25: "Notty" Problems (Page 37)

26. Finding six good prospects at the convention was better than our usual success rate.

    See Bug #26: Global *Which* (Page 38)

27. Programmers who always talk about the good old days bore the younger staff members.

   OR

Programmers who talk about the good old days always bore the younger staff members.

   See Bug #27: Squinting Modifier (Page 39)

28. Copies of the financial statement may be given only to members of the Finance Committee.

   See Bug #28: Misplaced Modifier (Page 40)

29. The new system will be dedicated to issuing benefit checks.

   See Bug #29: Excess Qualification (Page 41)

30. Their final offer was different from their first.

   See Bug #30: Faulty Prepositions (Page 42)

31. The boss talked about his own problems to Jones.

   OR

The boss said Jones had problems.

   See Bug #31: Obscure Antecedents (Page 43)

32. No one believes that the management will forget its promises.

   See Bug #32: Optional Words (Page 44)

BUG #1: CONFUSED PAIRS

Beware of words that sound alike and are often mistaken for each other. For example

    ACCEPT means *receive* or *take*.
    EXCEPT means *not including*.

    AFFECT (verb) means *influence*.
    EFFECT (verb) means *cause* or *effectuate*.

    ALTERNATE means *substitute*.
    ALTERNATIVE means *one of several ways* (originally one of two ways).

    APPRAISE means *rate* or *evaluate*.
    APPRISE means *inform*.

    AVERSE means *opposed to*.
    ADVERSE means *unfriendly* or *dangerous*.

    CONTINUAL means *often* and *intermittent*.
    CONTINUOUS means *all the time*.

    FORTUITOUS means *accidental*.
    FORTUNATE means *lucky*.

    LAY (verb) means *put* or *place* (lay, laid, laid).
    LIE (verb) means *rest* or *repose* (lie, lay, lain).

    LIMIT means *boundary* or *extent*.
    LIMITATION means *shortcoming* or *defect*.

    MASTERFUL means *domineering*, *overwhelming*.
    MASTERLY means *skillful*.

    SIMPLE means *uncomplicated* or *easy to understand*.
    SIMPLISTIC means *naive* or *shallow*.

Be on guard for "averse conditions" and "fortuitous accidents." Do not call something "simplistic" if you like it. And be careful about characterizing anyone's "limitations."

BUG #2: MISUSED TERMS

Beware of commonly misused terms. Whenever you suspect—even slightly—that you are misusing a word, look it up in a reliable dictionary. Here are some words that are misused daily:

Suspect Word	Wrong Meaning	Right Meaning
comprises	makes up	includes
decompose	disassemble	decay
due to	because	caused by
embattled	harassed	ready to fight
enormity	hugeness	evil
hopefully	we hope	with hope
infer	imply	deduce
presently	now	soon
transparent	invisible	obvious
verbal	oral	in words
verbiage	text, words	wasted words

BUG #3: OVERBLOWN NOUNS

Do not automatically choose long and fancy nouns when short, familiar nouns will do just as well.
Whenever you use a noun with three or more syllables, check to see if it can be replaced with a
shorter, lighter noun. For example

Replace This	With This
application, task	job
capability	ability
commencement	beginning
compensation, remuneration	pay
conceptualization	idea, draft, plan
condition, situation	state, status
determination	choice
finalization	end
implementation	start, use
indication	sign
interaction, interface	discussions
linkage	link
location	site, place
methodology	method
prioritization	ranking
requirement	need, wish
reservation	doubt
utilization	use

Of course, sometimes we all prefer the words on the left. But, unless there is some powerful reason,
choose one on the right.

BUG #4: COUNTERFEIT COINS

Do not make up new words unless there is no English word or phrase that means what you are trying to communicate. Sometimes words are created by "back formation"; so, the legitimate *attend* gives us the absurd *attendee*. (At least the word should have been *attender*.)

Beware, especially, of these counterfeits:

Counterfeit	Real
administrate	administer
attendee	participant
commentate	comment
deselect	reject
"heighth"	height
impact (verb)	affect
interviewee	respondent
irregardless	regardless
orientate	orient
preventative	preventive
reference (verb)	refer to
remediate	remedy
strategical	strategic
verbage	verbiage

Modern dictionaries often describe these counterfeits as "variants"—meaning that many people are prone to the error. *Preventative* is a variant of *preventive*. Generally, though, the only people who should feel comfortable with variant spellings and variant forms are variants.

BUG #5: SURPLUS NOUNS

Certain nouns have a way of being added to phrases without adding any meaning or precision. The most serious offenders are:

- approach
- area
- concept
- condition
- enviroment

- location
- problem
- situation
- type

No: He was interested in the distributed processing concept.
Yes: He was interested in distributed processing.

No: We are in an economic downturn situation.
Yes: We are in an economic downturn.

No: We have an employee absence problem.
Yes: We have too much employee absence.

No: They wanted a database type system.
Yes: They wanted a database system.

No: This accounting program is a less labor-intensive approach.
Yes: This accounting program is less labor-intensive.

No: Team leaders should meet in the dining-room area.
Yes: Team leaders should meet in the dining-room.

No: We want to hire someone with experience in an MVS environment.
Yes: We want to hire someone with experience in MVS.

NOTE: *Environment* **is so widely and imprecisely used these days that good writers will avoid it.**

BUG #6: DOUBLE-TALK

Avoid phrases that say the same thing twice. For example

Too Much	Better
repeat again	repeat
refer back	refer
consensus of opinion	opinion
staff-year of effort	staff-year
visible to the eye	visible
complete stop	stop
entirely complete	complete
integral part	part
active consideration	consideration
concatenated together	concatenated
past history	history
new innovation	innovation
exactly alike	alike
precisely the same	the same

These redundant phrases contain unnecessary words that merely repeat the meaning associated with the main term. All consideration is active, for instance. Only when you are using the term in an exceptional way do you need the extra qualifier. Thus, a stop is always complete, unless you tell us otherwise. And a part is always integral, unless you mean something else by it.

    No: The appendix refers back to the tutorial.
    Yes: The appendix refers to the tutorial.
       (NOTE: Never "references the")

BUG #7: SPACE-WASTERS

Avoid the habit of using extra words when you express measurements of distance, space, or volume.

For example

Instead of	Write
in length	long
in height	high
10 square feet of space	10 square feet
15 square meters of area	15 square meters
3 cubic yards of volume	3 cubic yards
distance of 4 kilometers	4 kilometers (away)
in a westward direction	westward
rectangular in shape	rectangular

No: Structures shall not be more than 100 meters in height.
Yes: Structures shall not be more than 100 meters high.
      (Watch out for "heighth")

No: The comet is approaching from a location 50,000,000 miles away.
Yes: The comet is approaching from 50,000,000 miles.

BUG #8: TIME-WASTERS

Express units and quantities of time as simply as possible. For example

Instead of	Write
period of time	time, period
interval of time	interval
twenty-minute period	twenty minutes
five months' duration	five months
three hours long	three hours
during periods of time	during
three hours of time	three hours

Avoid "calendar month" and "calendar year." Write just *month* or *year*—unless the word *calendar* is necessary to distinguish your statement from "person-month" or "staff-year."

And NEVER use the absurd expression "time frame"—an unclear term that usually just means schedule or deadline.

> No: This modification project, which will require a duration of three months, cannot be done under your time frame.
> Yes: This modification project, which will take three months, cannot be done by your deadline.

BUG #9: THROAT-CLEARERS

When speakers need a moment to find a word or phrase, they clear their throats (or use some other ploy). When writers are stuck, they use characteristic phrases and expressions: throat-clearers.

Be wary of such expressions as:

in order to	the nature of
in order for	the case of
for the reason that	relative to
it is apparent that	we really must
with a view to	relative to
in terms of	it is generally the case that

No: In order to classify my reactions, let me say that they are on the order of suggestions for improvement.

Yes: Think of my reactions as suggestions for improvement.

One of the most important differences between speech and writing is that when writing we have the opportunity—the obligation—to trim away these excesses. Nearly all first drafts contain clutter and excess, which is one reason why we all must edit.

BUG #10: *BECAUSE*-PHOBIA

Many writers, acting on misinformation from their schoolteachers, are afraid of the word *because*—especially at the beginning of a sentence. **NOTE: There is not now, nor has there ever been, a rule against using *because* at the beginning of a sentence!**

To avoid this nonexistent problem, many writers use *since* (acceptable, but often ambiguous), as (short for *inasmuchas* and somewhat too British for American writers), or *due to* (which means "caused by," not "because of," and is therefore unsuitable for the beginning of a sentence!). We also have *due to the fact that, for the reason that, based on the conclusion that*, and even weirder locutions.

> No: Since we hired our own illustrator, the manuals have improved.
> Yes: Because we hired our own illustrator, the manuals have improved.
> OR
> Yes: Ever since we hired our own illustrator, the manuals have improved.

> No: Due to the strike our installation was delayed.
> Yes: Because of the strike our installation was delayed.

> No: As the update had not been completed, we canceled the quarterly report.
> Yes: Because the update had not been completed, we canceled the quarterly report.

> No: The sponsor was worried since we were over budget.
> Yes: The sponsor was worried because we were over budget.

Other writers, fearful of starting with because, reverse the natural order of the because-therefore sentence.

> No: We changed contractors because of the complaints above.
> Yes: Because of the complaints above, we changed contractors.

In most cases, the "worried sponsor" sentence should read

> Yes: Because we were over budget, the sponsor was worried.

BUG #11: *DUE TO*

Ironically, to avoid *because* at the beginning of sentences (where it is allowed to appear), many writers choose *due to*, a phrase that cannot appear at the beginning of a sentence or clause.

The phrase *due to* is NOT a synonym for *because of*. *Due to* means *attributable to* or *caused by*. Generally, use it after the verb *to be* (*am, are, is, was, were, be*) or after what the grammarian calls a "linking" verb (such as *appears, seems, feels*).

No: Due to the number of mistakes, we are rewriting the manual.
Yes: Because of the number of mistakes, we are rewriting the manual.
        OR
Yes: The rewriting of the manual is due to the number of mistakes.

No: We have changed passwords due to the recent break-in.
Yes: We have changed passwords because of the recent break-in.
        OR
Yes: Because of the recent break-in, we have changed passwords.

No: The delay appears to be because of price problems.
Yes: The delay appears due to price problems.

BUG #12: *ABOUT*-PHOBIA

Do not be afraid of *about* in any of its meanings.

Write *about* instead of:

approximately	within the ballpark of
in the vicinity of	more or less
on the order of	in the range of
relative to	in connection with
regarding	pursuant to
re	reference
on the subject of	in relation to
relating to the subject of	respecting
in the matter of	in reference to
with regard to	with respect to

No: There were on the order of a hundred inquiries.
Yes: There were about a hundred inquiries.

No: Smith's report was in relation to offshore competition.
Yes: Smith's report was about offshore competition.

Of course, an occasional variation may be appropriate. Generally, though, write *about*.

BUG #13: *USE*-PHOBIA

Once, the word *utilize* meant "use for a profit"; it was a limited, specialized application of the word *use*. Today, though, *utilize* and *utilization* are nearly always ostentatious substitutes for *use*. Indeed, the word has been so abused that a good writer cannot feel safe that it will be understood when used correctly.

My advice: Stop writing *utilize*. Say *employ* if you want to avoid the phrase "using people." (Any day now, someone in a soap opera will accuse someone else by saying, "You utilized me.")

No: The company utilizes econometric models in its market forecasts.
Yes: The company uses econometric models in its market forecasts.

No: Our clerical staff is underutilized.
Yes: Our clerical staff is underworked.

No: We proposed the utilization of a stricter security system.
Yes: We proposed the use of a stricter security system.
    OR
Yes: We proposed a stricter security system.
    OR
Yes: We urged stricter security.

BUG #14: *NOW/THEN*-PHOBIA

Do not substitute long-winded or fancy expressions for now and then.

Write *NOW* Instead of	Write *THEN* Instead of
at this time	at that time
at this point	at that point
at this point in time	at that point in time
after further consideration	at that date
upon further reflection	as of that time
at present	up until that time
at the present time	during the past
as of this time	in that period
our current belief is	during that earlier time frame
as of today	within those earlier parameters
so far as we can see at this point in time	in the past

To avoid overuse of *now*, write *today*, *lately*, or *recently*.

To avoid overuse of *then*, write *earlier*, *later*, or *before*.

Never use *presently* for *now*; it means *soon*.

BUG #15: *CAN*-PHOBIA

Always distrust the words *capability* and *ability*. Usually, they are long-winded ways of avoiding the verb *can*.

> No: Our team does not have the ability to write a federal proposal.
> Yes: Our team cannot write a federal proposal.

> No: This program has a matrix rotation capability.
> Yes: This program can rotate a matrix.

> No: Their office has no fax capability.
> Yes: Their office cannot fax.
> > OR
> Yes: Their office has no fax machine.

Overuse by government and data processing professionals has nearly destroyed the word *capability*. Once it meant "potential"; today, no one knows whether it refers to current abilities, forthcoming features, or inherent possibilities. Good writers will avoid the word.

BUG #16: *MUST*-PHOBIA

Do not be afraid to write *must* (or *has to*) as an auxiliary verb.

Always examine sentences with such words as *required/requirement, responsible/responsibility,* or *necessary/necessity,* to see if a *must* will be clearer.

No: It is necessary to have complete documentation.
Yes: We must have complete documentation.

No: The operator on duty at 4 p.m. has the responsibility of logging off the system.
Yes: The operator on duty at 4 p.m. has to log off the system.

No: Updating these consumer loan accounts monthly is a mandatory procedure.
Yes: You must update these consumer loan accounts monthly.

No: It is the auditor's responsibility to schedule the visit.
Yes: The auditor has to schedule the visit.

Must and *has to* are used in procedures. Alternately, *should* or *ought* to are used in recommendations.

And *shall* is used in laws, policies, contracts, or any other document with the force of law.

BUG #17: *MAY/MIGHT*-PHOBIA

Do not be afraid to write *may* (or *might*) as an auxiliary verb. In modern American English, the distinction between the two terms grows less precise. Of course, *might* is the past form of *may* (I *may* finish. . . I might have finished. . .). When both are used in the present or future, *may* is generally used with events that are more likely to occur; *might* with events that have a smaller chance or that are in doubt:

> She may attend Stanford this fall.
> She might be their most talented freshman.

Such words as *likelihood* and *possibility* are usually signs that you should have used *may* or *might*.

> No: There is a possibility that they will bid against us.
> Yes: They may bid against us.

> No: There was some likelihood that they would have preferred to rent rather than buy.
> Yes: They might have preferred to rent rather than buy.

> No: Is there a probability that we can use some of the old inventory?
> Yes: Might we be able to use some of the old inventory?

BUG #18: *TO*-PHOBIA

Do not use three or four (or six or eight) words as a substitute for *to*.

> **Write *to* instead of**
> · in order to
> · so as to be able to
> · with a view to
> · as a way to
> · for the purpose of being able to
> · as a means to

In most cases, the word *to* alone will say what you mean. Of course, in those rare cases where these additional words carry a special meaning, leave them in.

No: In order to accelerate the project, we are using prototyping.
Yes: To accelerate the project, we are using prototyping.

No: We opened the project to bids with a view to being able to get a better price.
Yes: We opened the project to bids to get a better price.
        OR
Yes: To get a better price, we opened the project to bids.

BUG #19: *SO*-PHOBIA

So is a clear, functional, effective word. Because children are overly fond of the word, their teachers often scold them for using it at the start of a sentence. But there is no rule against its use, just as there is no rule against starting with *but*

Do not be afraid to use *so* in either of its two senses: as a synonym for *in order that* and as a simpler way of saying *therefore*.

So-I (*in order that, so as to be able, for the reason that*)

No: We revised the procedure in order that the operators would need fewer steps to generate the final reports.
Yes: We revised the procedure so the operators would need fewer steps to generate the final reports.

No: So as to be better able to detect unwarranted machine use, we added additional security features.
Yes: So we can detect unwarranted machine use, we added additional security features.

So-II (*thus, therefore, consequently, as a result*)

No: Thus, our conclusion is that we will use CASE tools.
Yes: So we conclude that we will use CASE tools.

No: Therefore, we cannot afford an additional console this year.
Yes: So, we cannot afford an additional console this year.

No: In view of these assessments and alternatives, we are choosing Colorado Springs.
Yes: So, we are choosing Colorado Springs.

BUG #20: *BY/WITH*-PHOBIA

Do not be afraid of *by* and *with*. They are much clearer and livelier than

- by means of
- by using
- utilizing
- through the use of
- via
- by employing
- by involving

No: Clear the database by means of a ZERO command.

Yes: Clear the database with a ZERO command.

No: Excessive delays in the changeover can be prevented through the use of early training.

Yes: Excessive delays in the changeover can be prevented by early training.

No: Utilizing a different file structure, this report could be run with much less CPU time.

Yes: With a different file structure, this report could be run with much less CPU time.

No: You can speed installation by the utilization of a prompt-driven installation program.

Yes: You can speed installation with a prompt-driven installation program.

BUG #21: *FOR*-PHOBIA

Don't ignore *for* in favor of such longer expressions as

- in order for
- for the purpose of
- to accomplish
- to ensure
- to allow
- to achieve
- to effectuate

No: In order for this report to be produced, you will need to link three files.
Yes: For this report you will need to link three files.

No: You usually need three commands to accomplish rotation of the drawing.
Yes: You usually need only three commands for rotation of the drawing.

No: To ensure security, we use a hierarchy of passwords.
Yes: For security, we use a hierarchy of passwords.

No: We set up the booth in order to achieve some recognition of our products.
Yes: We set up the booth for recognition of our products.

BUG #22: *IF*-PHOBIA

Use the word *if* in place of such ponderous expressions as *should it prove to be the case that*, or *in the event that*.

> No: In the event that there are blanks in one of the columns, display the arithmetic for that problem.
>
> Yes: If there are blanks in one of the columns, display the arithmetic for that problem.

> No: In those cases when the report is perfect, send it to the postscript printer.
>
> Yes: If the report is perfect, send it to the postscript printer.

> No: On those occasions when scientists are the main users of the system, FORTRAN is the best language.
>
> Yes: If scientists are the main users of the system, FORTRAN is the best language.

Sometimes, *when*, *whenever*, and *where* are also acceptable substitutes.

> Where there are blanks. . .
>
> When the report is perfect. . .
>
> Whenever scientists are the main users. . .

BUG #23: *OF*-PHOBIA

Use the word *of* instead of such ponderous expressions as

- derived from
- realized from
- noted in
- associated with
- inherent to
- obtained from

No: Notice the cost advantage derived from using optical character readers.

Yes: Notice the cost advantage of using optical character readers.

No: We decided to study the impact realized from our magazine advertisements.

Yes: We decided to study the impact of our magazine advertisements.

No: This report generator is free from the formatting problems noted in our first version.

Yes: This report generator is free from the formatting problems of our first version.

In general, avoid having two *of* phrases in a row:

No: The instructions are on the back of the box of the printer cable.

BUG #24: DIGITAL/ANALOG

Certain words, such as *fewer*, go with countable (digital, plural) objects; others, such as *less*, go with continuous (analog, singular) volumes and quantities.

The most commonly misused pairs are *less/fewer* and *amount/number*.

Less/Fewer

No: We had less bugs in this program.
Yes: We had fewer bugs in this program.
      OR
Yes: We had less trouble with this program.

Amount/Number

No: The new process increased the amount of breakdowns.
Yes: The new process increased the number of breakdowns.
      OR
Yes: The new process increased the amount of downtime.

The word *more* is the opposite of both *less* and *fewer*. Also, be careful of the words *much* (analog) and *many* (digital).

Much/Many

No: How much of the interruptions were our fault?
Yes: How many of the interruptions were our fault?
      OR
Yes: How much of the disruption was our fault?

BUG #25: "NOTTY" PROBLEMS

Not is a troublesome word. Be especially careful of two problems:

· confusing *not all* with *all. . . not*
· negating both parts of a compound

Not all

No: All of the old modules do not fit the new version.
Yes: Not all of the old modules fit the new version.

No: All accounting packages are not alike.
Yes: Not all accounting packages are alike.

Compound

No: New project managers do not learn from the mistakes of their predecessors and make all the
     same errors.
Yes: New project managers do not learn from the mistakes of their predecessors; instead, they
     make all the same errors.

Many editors try to remove *not*s, seeking some word that means "not x." Good writers avoid *not*—
except when they are making a strong denial. Use *not* when you believe it should be underscored for
emphasis. In fact, when you use the word spell it *NOT*; if the emphasis seems disproportionate,
perhaps you will want to recast the sentence with a different word.

NOTE: Spelling *not* with capital letters helps prevent us from overlooking it when we proofread. Many proofreading lapses involve the word *not*.

BUG #26: GLOBAL *WHICH*

In English the word *which* is usually attached to the word before it. It may, however, refer to an entire clause or idea that preceded it. This construction, although legal, is potentially dangerous and confusing. Careful writers will want to avoid it.

Legal but confusing:

The Department Manager was not told of the new password, which was foolish.

Better:

The Department Manager was not told of the new password, which fact was foolish. [Somewhat too British for American writers]

Not telling the Department Manager the new password was foolish.
   OR
Failing to tell the Department Manager the new password was foolish.

You may use the global *which* whenever there is no chance that the *which* will be incorrectly tied to the noun before it. In the sentence above, it sounds either as though the new password is the word FOOLISH or that there is something absurd about the word itself.

BUG #27: SQUINTING MODIFIER

Sometimes a word (usually an adverb) will be placed in such a way that we cannot tell which of two words it is modifying. We call these words "squinting" because we do not know which way they are looking.

No: Senior analysts who talk about the past continuously confuse novice programmers.
Yes: Senior analysts who talk continuously about the past confuse novice programmers.
     OR
Yes: Senior analysts who talk about the past are always confusing novice programmers.

BUG #28: MISPLACED MODIFIER

Certain modifiers are slippery; they slide into the wrong position in the sentence. The most dangerous are *only*, *almost*, *already*, *even*, *just*, *nearly*, *merely*, and *always*.

Almost

No: They almost worked five years on that system.
Yes: They worked almost five years on that system.

Just

No: They just wanted a 30-day extension.
Yes: They wanted just a 30-day extension.

Only

No: The database only contains the year-end summaries for 1980–1985.
Yes: The database contains only the year-end summaries for 1980–1985. (Not the monthly or quarterly summaries)
OR
Yes: The database contains the year-end summaries only for 1980–1985. (Not for 1975–1979)

These small words can, through misplacement, alter the emphasis or meaning of a sentence. Consider these examples:

The union wants to buy the company's assets.
Only the union wants to buy the company's assets.
The union wants only to buy the company's assets.
The union wants to buy only the company's assets.

In general, these slippery descriptors should appear just before the terms they modify.

BUG #29: EXCESS QUALIFICATION

Do not modify or qualify words that don't need to be modified or qualified. For example

Excessive	Better
totally committed	committed
completely devoted	devoted
utterly rejected	rejected
utterly unique	unique
perfectly clear	clear
completely compatible	compatible
completely accurate	accurate
quite precise	precise
quite innovative	innovative
radically new	new

The only time to qualify these terms is when they are used in a special or odd sense. *Dedicated* is always total, and *complete* is always entire. (Some overzealous writers use "30% complete" to mean they are about to begin, while "90% complete" means they have just begun.)

There is no such thing as *slightly devoted*, or *somewhat unique*, or *relatively precise*. The expression *most random* is nonsense, as is *partially committed*.

BUG #30: FAULTY PREPOSITIONS

Many English idioms contain prepositions that are hard to keep straight, even for native speakers.

Compare

Compare *to* means to point out similarities.
Compare *with* means to measure against.

Yes: They always compare him to his predecessor.
Yes: How does Release 3 compare with Release 2?

Concur

You concur *with* someone.
You concur *in* an idea or assertion.

Yes: We concur with the director of training.
Yes: The director of training concurs in the plan to merge publications and training.

Disappoint

You are disappointed *in* someone.
You are disappointed *with* something.

Yes: I am disappointed in this consultant.
Yes: I am disappointed with this study.

Graduate

Graduate takes the preposition *from*.

No: When did he graduate Northwestern?
Yes: When did he graduate from Northwestern?

Different

Different takes *from*, not *than*.

No: My read/write privileges are different than yours.
Yes: My read/write privileges are different from yours.

BUG #31: OBSCURE ANTECEDENTS

See that every pronoun points clearly to some noun or noun phrase. Pronouns without clear antecedents are treacherous for the reader.

His (or Her)

No: He told the controller his phone was not working.
> WHOSE PHONE?

Yes: He told the controller that the controller's phone was not working.

They

No: Operator's manuals should not be given to new employees until they have been date-stamped.
> WHO OR WHAT IS TO BE DATE-STAMPED?

Yes: Operator's manuals should not be given to new employees until these manuals have been date-stamped.

It

No: The computer uses CD-ROM. It is worth the price.
> WHAT IS WORTH THE PRICE?

Yes: The computer uses CD-ROM, a storage technology that is worth the price.

This

No: Calculus is a prerequisite for the course, but this can be waived.
> WHAT CAN BE WAIVED?

Yes: Calculus is a prerequisite for the course, but this requirement can be waived.

Lacking a clear antecedent, a pronoun is presumed to refer to the closest eligible noun that precedes it. (This "default" rule can produce some weird meanings, like the "date-stamped employees.")

Although it may be inelegant, repeating the noun is sometimes the only solution.

BUG #32: OPTIONAL WORDS

When a word is truly unnecessary, cut it. Most so-called optional words, though, make the sentence clearer or easier to follow. The two most common cases are (1) *that* at the beginning of a noun clause used as an object and (2) the first two words in a nonrestrictive clause.

That-clauses

In the sentence below, *that* signals the beginning of a long clause and, thereby, helps orient the reader:

> The sales rep claimed (that) distributed processing would be more cost-effective than the current configuration.

In the next example, leaving out that sets the readers on the wrong tack:

> Everyone in the industry believed (that) the RFP was wired.
> (Without *that*, it sounds as though everyone believed the RFP; in fact, though, everyone believed it was deceiving.)

Nonrestrictive clauses

The safest words to cut are those optional items at the beginning of a nonrestrictive clause—that is, a parenthetical expression set off with commas. For example

> The terms and conditions, (which are) described in Chapter 6, must be followed.
> The candidate, (who is) an MIT man, is overqualified for this position.

If there is any possibility that cutting the optional word will make the sentence harder to read, do not cut!

> No: I don't believe the average physician will take the trouble to use this information system.
> Yes: I don't believe that the average physician will take the trouble to use this new information system.

VERBS,
In Particular

VERB PROBLEMS

These sentences have verb problems. Look for

- nouns that can be turned into verbs
- passives that can be turned into actives
- any other ways to make the verbs lively and interesting

33. They cannot do a verification of the data until you make a decision about the new password.

_____

(Remedy: Page 49)

34. They could not furnish us with an explanation of the problem.

_____

(Remedy: Page 49)

35. Rectangle formation can be realized in three ways.

_____

(Remedy: Page 49)

36. This chapter serves to define the five main commands.

_____

(Remedy: Page 49)

37. After each transaction, determine whether it is necessary to retain a hard copy of the output.

_____

(Remedy: Page 49)

38. Extensive editing can be invoked by the user.

_____

(Remedy: Page 49)

39. In the next chapter the error messages are explained.

_____

(Remedy: Page 49)

40. A meeting was held and the decision was reached not to give the attorney an answer.

_____

(Remedy: Page 49)

41. It was determined that in the next test ease of operation would be evaluated.

_____

(Remedy: Page 50)

42. Please advise headquarters of our expansion decision.

_____

(Remedy: Page 50)

43. Testing the column arithmetic should occur before generating any reports.

_____

(Remedy: Page 50)

44. There will not be enough time to completely debug the system.

_____

(Remedy: Page 50)

45. The model is not flexible enough to do simulations with.

_____

(Remedy: Page 50)

VERB REMEDIES

33. They cannot verify the data until you decide on the new password.

    See Bug #33: Smothered Verbs-Basic (Page 51)

34. They could not explain the problem.

    See Bug #34: Smothered Verbs-Intermediate (Page 52)

35. You can form rectangles in three ways.

    See Bug #35: Smothered Verbs-Advanced (Page 53)

36. This chapter defines the five main commands.

    See Bug #36: Weak Servants (Page 54)

37. After each transaction, decide whether to keep a hard copy of the output.

    See Bug #37: Overblown Verbs (Page 55)

38. The user can invoke extensive editing.

    See Bug #38: Passive with *By* (Page 56)

39. The next chapter explains the error messages.

    See Bug #39: Passives with *In, At, For*. . . (Page 57)

40. They met and decided not to answer the attorney.

    See Bug #40: Passive with No Actor (Page 58)

41. They decided to test ease of operation next.

　　　See Bug #41: Passive with *It*　(Page 59)

42. Please advise headquarters that we have decided to expand.

　　　See Bug #42: Verbs Disguised as Nouns　(Page 60)

43. Before you generate any reports, test the column arithmetic.

　　　See Bug #43: Verbs Disguised as Gerunds　(Page 61)

44. There will not be enough time to debug the system completely.

　　OR

　There will not be enough time to debug the system.

　　　See Bug #44: "Split Infinitives"　(Page 62)

45. The model is not flexible enough for simulations.
　　　See Bug #45: Verbs with Prepositional Tails (Page 63)

BUG #33: SMOTHERED VERBS—BASIC

From the time we are schoolchildren we are encouraged to write as many words as possible, and to be as impressive as possible in our choice of vocabulary. If we succeed, we are rewarded with high grades and praise.

Unfortunately, pursuing either of these objectives seriously harms our writing. And the most common device used to these ends is "the smothered verb," a practice in which a verb is converted to a noun and made the object of a less interesting verb. For instance, *judge* becomes *make a judgment on*.

The first category of smothered verb is a phrase beginning with *have* or *make*.

Instead of	Write
have an objection	object
have knowledge of	know
have reservations about	doubt
have a suspicion	suspect
have a concern	care, worry
make a distinction	distinguish
make a recommendation	recommend
make a suggestion	suggest
make a proposal	propose

No: I did not have sufficient knowledge of the problem to make a proposal regarding a new system.

Yes: I did not know enough about the problem to propose a new system.

BUG #34: SMOTHERED VERBS—INTERMEDIATE

Smothered verbs can be made in many ways. Although the most common forms use *have* and *make*, there are also hundreds of expressions using such words as *give*, *reach*, and *do*.

Instead of	Write
give an answer to	answer
give an apology	apologize
give a justification for	justify
reach a conclusion	conclude
reach a decision	decide
reach an end	end, finish
reach an agreement	agree
do an inspection of	inspect, check
do a draft of	draft
raise an objection	object
hold the opinion	believe
send an invitation to	invite
hold a meeting	meet
furnish an explanation for	explain
furnish a solution for	solve
form a plan regarding	plan

No: These receipts furnish no explanation for your expenses.
Yes: These receipts do not explain your expenses.

No: We held a meeting and reached a decision to send him an invitation to the bidders' conference.
Yes: We met and decided to invite him to the bidders' conference.

BUG #35: SMOTHERED VERBS—ADVANCED

In the writing of technical professionals, we also find an especially ornate and complicated form of smothered verb, using such words as *accomplish*, *achieve*, *realize*, or even *effectuate*. To make things worse, this last group often appears in the passive voice of the verb.

Instead of	Write
separation was accomplished	they separated
a profit was realized	they profited
effectuate a system start-up	start up the system
file linkage was achieved	the files were linked
exhibit improvement	improve
evidence size reduction	shrink, reduce

No: A tendency to short-out was evidenced by these circuit-packs.
Yes: These circuit-packs tended to short-out.

No: The calculations to project interim costs are accomplished entirely in TREND.
Yes: TREND calculates the projections of interim costs.
        OR
Yes: TREND projects the interim costs.

Clearly, these tortuous expressions are supposed to impress readers. But they do not. Quite the contrary, they often suggest that the writer is embarrassed or uncomfortable, perhaps even deceitful.

BUG #36: WEAK SERVANTS

Be careful of the close cousin of the smothered verb: the weak servant. These wordy constructions feature such terms as *serve, use, conduct, carry out*, and *perform*. Here are some typical examples:

Serve

No: This design serves to explain the three stages of the project.
Yes: This design explains the three stages of the project.

Use

No: The light pen is used to correct errors in the array on the screen.
Yes: The light pen corrects errors in the array on the screen.

Conduct

No: The agency will conduct an investigation of the purchase.
Yes: The agency will investigate the purchase.

Carry Out

No: Can we carry out the inspection of this landfill before November?
Yes: Can we inspect this landfill before November?

Perform

No: Comparison of the actual and projected is performed within the software.
Yes: The software compares the actual with the projected.

BUG #37: OVERBLOWN VERBS

Don't use big verbs for the sake of showing off or sounding more "technical."

Instead of	Write
communicate, interface with	speak, tell, write, discuss
determine, ascertain	see, decide
endeavor, essay, attempt	try
finalize, terminate	end
formulate, fabricate, construct	make
indicate, reveal, present, suggest	show, tell, say
initiate, commence	begin
inspect, ascertain, investigate	check
modify, alter, redesign	change
offer, present	give
possess, maintain	have
realize, appreciate	know
represents, seems	is
require, necessitate, mandate	need
retain, preserve	keep, save
select, opt for	pick
transmit, disseminate	send
utilize, employ	use

No: They indicated that the project would be delivered on time.

Yes: They said the project would be delivered on time.

No: By June, we will be able to determine whether the fix is adequate.

Yes: By June, we will see whether the fix is adequate.

No: Be sure to communicate your comments to S&E.

Yes: Be sure to send your comments to S&E.

Use the longer verbs only if they have a shade of meaning that suits the sentence more precisely.

Otherwise, choose the simpler form.

BUG #38: PASSIVE WITH *BY*

In the passive voice of the verb, the subject is acted upon instead of acting. Be careful not to write in the passive voice unless you have some compelling reason to do so.

The passive voice will usually make your sentences longer, clumsier, harder to understand, and more vulnerable to other errors of grammar and style. Instructions in the passive voice are harder to follow than instructions in the active. Recommendations in the passive have less force than those in the active.

In the most common form of the passive, we reverse the natural sequence of the sentence and put the actor or subject into a phrase beginning with *by*.

> No: A Preventive Maintenance Manual is left on the site by the field engineer.
> Yes: The field engineer leaves a Preventive Maintenance Manual on the site.

> No: Flexibility is not exhibited by the procedure.
> Yes: The procedure is inflexible (or rigid).

The only time you will choose deliberately this passive form is when you want to put the true subject or actor at the end of the sentence (for emphasis), or when you want to avoid a dangling construction. In general, presume against your first-draft passives. Although some will remain, most will not survive a close reading.

BUG #39: PASSIVE WITH *IN, AT, FOR*. . .

In other passive constructions, the true subject or actor is concealed in a prepositional phrase beginning with *in, at, for, with,* or *through.* In the most irksome case, the prepositional phrase introduces the sentence.

In

No: In the next chapter the error messages are explained.
Yes: The next chapter explains the error messages.

At

No: At six of the campuses, facilities management contractors are used.
Yes: Six of the campuses use facilities management contractors.

For

No: For managers without formal training in accounting a special training module is needed.
Yes: Managers without formal training in accounting need a special training module.

With

No: With patients who smoke treatment with a higher dose is indicated.
Yes: Treat patients who smoke with a higher dose.

BUG #40: PASSIVE WITH NO ACTOR

In some passive sentences there is no mention of the true actor or subject. Sometimes such sentences are used to make statements in which it does not matter who the real subject is. (The last sentence is an example.) For example, the "Materials and Methods" section of a scientific paper, and sometimes the "Abstract," gain little by repeating "the investigators" in each sentence.

In other, less defensible cases, though, writers unwilling to assert themselves, or to accept responsibility for a claim, will make themselves invisible.

> No: Weaknesses were unexpectedly discovered during the third phase of study.
>> WHO DISCOVERED THE WEAKNESSES?

> No: The transition is intended to produce no disruption ofservice.
>> WHO IS MAKING THIS PROMISE?

> No: Your application has been rejected.
>> WHO REJECTED IT?

Notice the tone of evasiveness, the lack of personal accountability, in the following sentences:

> This method is no longer recognized as the safest.
> The Shipping Department was the acknowledged cause of the error.
> ACME is purported to be the least expensive.

Again, the maker of these allegations should be forthright, prepared to defend them—not hiding within the passive syntax.

BUG #41: PASSIVE WITH *IT*

One of the most characteristic signs of weak technical writing is the sentence that begins with an It-passive. These introductory clauses can usually be scratched out without any loss of meaning. Otherwise, replace them with active constructions.

Avoid such openings as

- It has been determined that...
- It can be seen that...
- It was found that...
- It was generally held that...
- It is believed that...

No: It has been determined that we will bid on the RFP.
Yes: We decided to bid on the RFP.
         OR
Yes: We will bid on the RFP.

Be cautious of any sentence beginning with *it is, it has*, or *it was*, whether or not the verb is passive. Although an occasional use of such sentences is acceptable, their overuse is suffocating. Those who prefer them are trying to make their writing sound more formal, and also to avoid personal pronouns. But *I* is the only problematical pronoun in technical communication; there is no need to run from *we* or *they*.

BUG #42: VERBS DISGUISED AS NOUNS

Often, when the verb in the sentence is to be (*is*, *are*, *was*, *were*, *be*) there is a noun nearby that would make a more lively and interesting verb.

No: Their decision was to expand, rather than replace.
Yes: They decided to expand, rather than replace.

No: Their approach was a separation of the personnel and payroll files.
Yes: They approached it by separating the personnel and payroll files.
     OR
Yes: They separated the personnel and payroll files.

No: This technique is an expansion of the original security system.
Yes: This technique expands the original security system.

Any time a key noun in a sentence ends in -*tion*, -*sion*, -*ment*, or -*ing*, there may be a verb hiding in that noun. For example

No: The first step in the procedure is the attachment of the grounding lead.
Yes: The first step in the procedure is to attach the grounding lead.

No: The hardest task is completion of the application.
Yes: The hardest task is to complete the application.

BUG #43: VERBS DISGUISED AS GERUNDS

A gerund is a form of the verb that ends in *ing* and acts as a noun. In the sentence "Running is good for you!" *running* is a gerund and the subject of the sentence.

Although gerunds are fine, clear, useful words, be careful that your gerund subjects or gerund objects are not concealing a more interesting verb. For example

> No: Logging-in is the next step after checking the acoustic coupler.
> Yes: After you check the acoustic coupler, log in.

> No: To prevent loss of data, operators use the backing-up procedure every five minutes.
> Yes: To prevent loss of data, operators back-up data every five minutes.

There is nothing wrong with gerunds. They are legitimate and often desirable. Merely be alert to cases—especially in instructions and directives—where the gerund is obscuring an interesting, direct verb.

BUG #44: "SPLIT INFINITIVES"

An infinitive is a form of the verb that begins with *to* and ends with a verb, for example, *to choose, to go,* or, in the passive, *to be selected, to be erased.* Many editors and readers object to "splitting the infinitive"—placing a modifier between to and the verb in the infinitive. They complain about such expressions as to *entirely evaluate* or *to be quickly lifted.* Thus, split infinitives are dangerous for the amateur writer—even though they do not violate any rule of English grammar.

The problem remains, though: Many readers with a slim knowledge of style insist that split infinitives are wrong. To avoid making your style too "visible," then, you are better off avoiding them.

To correct a split infinitive you may either (1) remove the modifier, (2) relocate the modifier, or (3) find a better verb that takes away the need for the modifier.

Remove

No: I intend to entirely finish this report today.
Yes: I intend to finish this report today.

Relocate

No: To boldly go where no man has gone before...
Yes: To go boldly where no man has gone before...

Replace the Verb

No: They have not been able to totally learn the language.
Yes: They have not been able to master the language.

Of course, if you really believe that the split form is the clearest and best form, you may decide to deliberately use it.

BUG #45: VERBS WITH PREPOSITIONAL TAILS

Most people know that you should not end a sentence with a preposition. Unfortunately, though, many English verbs have prepositions attached, and these attachments tend to appear at the ends of sentences and clauses.

If possible, choose some other verb when you discover that your first choice forces you to end with a preposition.

No:	Here is a problem we should attend to.
Stiff:	Here is a problem to which we should attend.
Formal:	Let us attend to this problem.
Best:	Here is a problem we should address.

Like the "split infinitive," the terminal preposition is a favorite complaint of people who understand little of the Teutonic origins of English verb forms. To reduce the risk of offending these sometimes powerful readers, be careful of verbs like these:

- work on
- listen to
- open up

- put up with
- make a fool of
- grant the truth of

Of course, if you really want to emphasize the preposition, you may deliberately put it at the end. Your reader will surely notice it!

PHRASES

PHRASE PROBLEMS

Each of the sentences below has at least one awkward or long-winded phrase. Improve the sentences in any way you can.

46. This file keeps track of the task responsibility assignment changes.

_____

(Remedy: Page 68)

47. The comptroller hired a short contracts expert.

_____

(Remedy: Page 68)

48. I have the résumés for four promising programmers on my desk.

_____

(Remedy: Page 68)

49. The bottom line is that John's proposal is not a viable alternative.

_____

(Remedy: Page 68)

50. There are no manuals which are available at this time for the customer.

_____

(Remedy: Page 68)

51. The first test was without a flaw.

_____

(Remedy: Page 68)

PHRASE REMEDIES

46. This file tracks changes in the assignment of responsibility.

   See Bug #46: Strings of Nouns (Page 69)

47. The comptroller hired an expert on short contracts.

   See Bug #47: Stacks of Modifiers (Page 70)

48. On my desk are the résumés of four promising programmers.

   See Bug #48: Misplaced Descriptive Phrases (Page 71)

49. In conclusion, John's proposal is unworkable.

   See Bug #49: Clichés and Vogue Phrases (Page 72)

50. There are no manuals available now for the customer.

   See Bug #50: Phrases into Words (Page 73)

51. The first test was flawless.

   See Bug #51: Phrases into Suffixes (Page 74)

BUG #46: STRINGS OF NOUNS

One of the most typical bugs in technical writing in general, and computer writing in particular, is the noun string (whoops, string of nouns!).

No writer can be understood who writes in strings of nouns, that is, two or more nouns in a row. Even a two-word string like *management option* could mean

- an option available to management
- one of several ways to manage
- the choice of having management or not

Instead of	Write
problem responsibility changes	changes in the assignment of responsibility
graphics construction language	language for constructing graphics
component reference designators	designators for referring to components
stability evaluation manager	manager to evaluate stability
operator-induced failure-rate increase problem	an undesirable increase in the rate of failures attributable to operators' errors
marketing action analysis	analysis of market actions
cardholder file	file of people holding cards

Noun strings are tolerable when they are the names of systems, or parts of systems (local area network conversion protocol), and when they are fully explained the first time they are introduced. In other contexts, though, they are cryptic and, therefore, dangerous.

BUG #47: STACKS OF MODIFIERS

Be careful of stacked modifiers (adjectives and adverbs). When two or more modifiers appear before the same noun, the meaning of the phrase is usually clear only to the writer. Be especially careful of cases in which the first descriptor could modify either the second descriptor or the noun. For example, what exactly is a "buried cable engineer"? (And how does one breathe?)

Instead of	Write
non-computer background personnel	personnel without backgrounds in computers
contiguous sector output	output from contiguous sectors
ad hoc reporting capability	ability to generate ad hoc reports
typical user interface problem areas	areas in which users typically have problems with the interface
long-range failure prevention program	long-range program for preventing failures
obsolete operator's manual	operator's manual that is obsolete OR manual for obsolete operators

Sometimes, these phrases are made clearer with hyphens that consolidate the modifiers into units. So, *more-effective reports* eliminates the ambiguity in *more effective reports*.

More often, though, hyphens do not solve the problem. The punctuation refines the meaning only for the reader who already understands the phrase. The naive reader will still be confused.

BUG #48: MISPLACED DESCRIPTIVE PHRASES

Descriptive phrases—especially those beginning with prepositions like *as, with, in, of, by, on, from*—should cling to the terms they describe. The greater the separation, the greater the ambiguity or potential for misinterpretation. Usually, the best location for the phrase is right after the term it describes; occasionally, just before.

> No: I wrote my evaluation of the new VDT in the quarterly report.
> Yes: I wrote in the quarterly report my evaluation of the new VDT.
> > OR
> Yes: In the quarterly report I wrote my evaluation of the new VDT.

> No: Notify the manager of breakdowns in accordance with department rules.
> Yes: In accordance with department rules, notify the manager of breakdowns.

Also be careful of placing two or more descriptive phrases in a row, especially when they begin with the same word.

> No: He sketched the new system on the backs of several envelopes on the way to the office.
> Yes: On the way to the office, he sketched the new system on the backs of several envelopes.

BUG #49: CLICHÉS AND VOGUE PHRASES

Avoid phrases and expressions that you are tired of reading or hearing, unless they happen to be the most correct and precise way to say what you want to say. The vogue word for these terms is *buzzwords*. For example

Terms	Phrases
actionable	fine tune
actualize	couldn't care less
ballpark	ground zero
concept	square one
hi-tech	touch base with
humongous	ramp-up time
impact (as a verb)	not rocket science
innovative	bottom-line
input	user-friendly
interface (as a verb)	high roller
leverage (as a verb)	best (worse) case scenario
proactive	rock and a hard place
scenario	team player
system	lion's share
team	
viable	

The trouble with vogue terms and phrases is that, first, no one is quite sure what they mean and, second, no one pays attention to them when they are spoken or written. (Also, they often go out of fashion before the document goes out of use, making them seem rather old-fashioned!)

Similarly, avoid poor and mixed figures of speech, like these terrible examples below:

Let's not fuel the fires of galloping inflation.
We backed him to the hilt when the chips were down.
It's time to gird up our resources.
Get a more tightly focused handle on the problem.

BUG #50: PHRASES INTO WORDS

Try not to use a phrase where a single word will do. For example

Instead of	Write
to all appearances	apparently
a possibility that	possibly, perhaps
as is clear from the above	clearly
for the most part	usually
in an incompetent manner	incompetent(ly)
with confidence	confident(ly)

No: As is obvious, the contractor is now in default.
Yes: Obviously, the contractor is now in default.

No: They were hoping to hire a manager with experience.
Yes: They were hoping to hire an experienced manager.

BUG #51: PHRASES INTO SUFFIXES

Sometimes you can improve a sentence by converting a phrase of several words into a simple suffix. The suffixes most useful in this case are *-less*, *-ly*, and *-ing*.

> No: The tests were run without a flaw.
> Yes: The tests were run flawlessly.

> No: The error message describes what went wrong in a very explicit fashion.
> Yes: The error message describes explicitly what went wrong.

> No: The number of reviewers who approved the publishing system we just bought gives us a sense of reassurance.
> Yes: The number of reviewers who approved the publishing system we just bought is reassuring.

When making these conversions, be careful of stacked modifiers. If converting the phrase to a suffix will create an awkward string of modifiers, stay with the original phrase.

SENTENCES

SENTENCE PROBLEMS

The sentences below need work. Look out for

- phrases in the wrong sequence
- clauses that are connected illogically
- series of terms that are not parallel
- extra words

NOTE: As you correct these sentences, do not turn one sentence into two. Except for sentence 65, none of these sentences contains so much information that it should be made into two or more sentences. (Sentence 65, as you will see, does have too much in it for one sentence to handle.)

52. Quarterly updates can be expected hereafter.

_____

(Remedy: Page 81)

53. The feasibility of making the transition in a single weekend should be noted.

_____

(Remedy: Page 81)

54. As an experienced programmer, my Department Chief gives me very little supervision.

_____

(Remedy: Page 81)

55. When logging in, the sheet must be filled accurately.

_____

(Remedy: Page 81)

56. To find the infirmary, red flags have been posted every thirty feet along the route.

_____

(Remedy: Page 81)

57. Do not service the copier while eating or drinking.

_____

(Remedy: Page 81)

58. Unfortunately, all the screens were bit-mapped.

_____

(Remedy: Page 81)

59. The report was short, logical and reading it was easy.

_____

(Remedy: Page 81)

60. The product had five faults:

    1. Not enough time to clean input data.
    2. All error messages were sent to the department manager.
    3. Too much rounding-off of time data.
    4. Coded column headings in the output.
    5. No one was sure of the distribution list.

_____

_____

_____

_____

(Remedy: Page 82)

61. The main advantages of the new accounting program are faster billing and how it analyzes speed-of-payment.

_____

_____

(Remedy: Page 82)

62. A decision to purchase the APEX inventory does not require corporate approval, since it is part of a previously established program.

_____

_____

(Remedy: Page 82)

63. There are three reasons we have for preferring a distributed system.

_____

(Remedy: Page 82)

64. It is not enough to give just the total price for the job.

_____

(Remedy: Page 82)

65. This is to notify you that exercise assignment notices are allocated among Jones, Smith & Doe customer short option positions pursuant to an automated procedure which randomly selects from among all customer short option positions, including positions established on the day of the assignment, those contracts which are subject to exercise.

_____

_____

_____

(Remedy: Page 82)

66. This software has two flaws. The first is its difficulty to use. The second is cost.

_____

(Remedy: Page 83)

67. The first step is preparation of a list of parts which are to be scrapped.

_____

(Remedy: Page 83)

68. We need a cooling system that does not make any noise whatsoever.

_____

(Remedy: Page 83)

SENTENCE REMEDIES

52. Hereafter, expect updates quarterly.

     See Bug #52: Backwards Sentences (Page 84)

53. We may be able to make the transition in a single weekend.

     See Bug #53: Empty Predicates (Page 85)

54. As an experienced programmer, I get very little supervision from the Department Chief.

     See Bug #54: Dangling Introductory Phrases (Page 86)

55. When logging in, you must fill the sheet accurately.

     OR

When logging in, (you) fill the sheet accurately.

     See Bug #55: Dangling Introductory Participles (Page 87)

56. To find the infirmary, visitors should follow the red flags posted every thirty feet along the route.

     See Bug #56: Dangling Introductory Infinitives (Page 88)

57. Do not service the copier while you are eating or drinking.

     See Bug #57: Dangling Ends (Page 89)

58. Unfortunately, all the screens were bit-mapped—not character-based, as our program requires.

     See Bug #58: Incomplete Contrasts (Page 90)

59. The report was short, logical, and readable.

     See Bug #59: Faulty Parallel—Short List (Page 91)

60. The product had five faults:

    1. Not enough time to clean input data
    2. Not enough information in the column headings of the output
    3. Not enough direction for the distribution list
    4. Too many messages sent to the department manager
    5. Too much rounding-off of data

    See Bug #60: Faulty Parallel—Long List (Page 92)

61. The main advantages of the new accounting program are faster billing and faster analysis of speed-of-payment.

    See Bug #61: Faulty Parallel—Compounds (Page 93)

62. Because APEX is part of a previously established program, a decision to purchase the APEX inventory does not need corporate approval.

    See Bug #62: Inverted Complex Sentences (Page 94)

63. We prefer a distributed system for three reasons.

    OR

We have three reasons for preferring a distributed system.

    See Bug #63: *There*-Sentences   (Page 95)

64. Giving just the total price for the job is not enough.

    See Bug #64: *It*-Sentences (Page 96)

65. This is to notify you that Jones, Smith & Doe uses an automated procedure to allocate exercise assignment notices (?) among its customer short option positions (?). This procedure draws randomly a set of contracts that are subject to exercise. It selects from all the customer short option positions—even from those established on the same day as the assignment.

    See Bug #65: Marathon Sentences (Page 97)

66. This software has two flaws; it is too hard to use and too expensive.

    OR

  This software has two flaws: its difficulty and its price.

    See Bug #66: Primer Sentences (Page 98)

67. The first step is to prepare a list of parts to be scrapped.

    See Bug #67: Clauses into Phrases (Page 99)

68. We need a silent cooling system.

    See Bug #68: Clauses into Words (Page 100)

BUG #52: BACKWARDS SENTENCES

Contrary to what you may believe, and contrary to what you might have been taught, the new, important, interesting information in a sentence should appear **at the end**. When we are composing first drafts, though, we tend to blurt out the interesting material at the beginning. Instead, think of a sentence as a story that builds in suspense and reaches a climax. Put the surprise last.

No: The end of a sentence is the place where the interesting information should appear.
Yes: The place in a sentence where the interesting information should appear is at the end.

No: The detailed analysis of trends and how they affect the business of the company is the purpose of the database.
Yes: The purpose of the database is to analyze trends and how they affect the business of the company.

No: Morale improvement is the most noticeable effect of the new telephone system.
Yes: The most noticeable effect of the new telephone system is improved morale.

Usually, editing the sentence to achieve this proper order will also smooth the transition to the next sentence. (The most interesting part of Sentence 1 is usually the trigger for Sentence 2.)

NOTE: More than the other bugs in this collection, the backwards sentence needs **editing**. That is, even the best writers make this error frequently in their first drafts. But the extra effort is undeniably rewarded: Learning to put the "payload" of the sentence last will have a dramatic effect on your powers of communication. This device alone can make all the difference between writing that bores the reader and writing that engages the reader's attention.

BUG #53: EMPTY PREDICATES

When we are composing, we often jam all the interesting information into the subject of the sentence and leave nothing for the predicate. Although these sentences are grammatically correct (they do have a predicate), they are awkward and dull. Such predicates as *exist*, *is provided*, *is worthy of mention*, and *is to be noted* are examples of the problem.

No: The need for better computer equipment in the high schools exists.
Yes: The high schools need better computer equipment.

No: Printing of user directories showing creation date and time is provided.
Yes: The system prints user directories that show the date and time of creation.

No: The possibility of producing the product locally is to be noted.
Yes: We can produce the product locally.

No: The desirability of shortening the loan period is worthy of mention.
Yes: We should shorten the loan period.

Sentences with empty predicates often have subject nouns ending in the syllables *-tion*, *-ment*, or *-ing*. Look for them in your own first drafts.

NOTE: If you put the main part of the sentence at the end, you will be unlikely to make this error.

BUG #54: DANGLING INTRODUCTORY PHRASES

An introductory phrase—a phrase that precedes the main clause of a sentence—should refer to (or modify) the noun that appears at the beginning of the main clause. Unfortunately, it will refer to that noun whether or not you intend it.

No: With more than 500 employees engaged in research and development, there is no aspect of modern computer science that is not in the company's expertise.

Yes: With more than 500 employees engaged in research and development, the company has expertise in every phase of computer science.

No: As an example of carelessness, the manager cited the report of the maintenance contractor.

Yes: As an example of carelessness, the report of the maintenance contractor earned the notice of the manager.

OR

Yes: The report of the maintenance contractor, according to the manager, is an example of carelessness.

No: As one of our brightest trainees, we are sending you to ADA school.

Yes: As one of our brightest trainees, you are a nominee for ADA school.

OR

Yes: Because you are one of our brightest trainees, we are sending you to ADA school.

BUG #55: DANGLING INTRODUCTORY PARTICIPLES

When there is a participle in the introductory phrase, the agent of the action in that participle should be the subject of the sentence and must appear immediately after the comma used to set off the phrase.

No: Wishing to analyze the failures of the project, a meeting was held between the sponsor and the contractor.

DID THE MEETING WISH?

Yes: Wishing to analyze the failures of the project, the sponsor and contractor met.

No: When initializing the system with a coldstart, a tape containing the operating system software is loaded.

DOES THE TAPE INITIALIZE THE SYSTEM?

Yes: When initializing the system with a coldstart, the operator loads a tape containing the operating software.

OR

Yes: When initializing the system with a coldstart, (you) load a tape containing the operating software.

No: Having finished my lunch, the PM called me to his office.

DID THE PM EAT YOUR LUNCH?

Yes: After lunch, the PM called me to his office.

There are some exceptions. Certain widely used expressions, even though they have participles in them, become "absolute" (that is, nonmodifying) constructions. Phrases like *considering your objections*, *given these problems*, *speaking of networks*, and *overlooking the price* may appear at the beginning of a sentence regardless of their link to the subject.

BUG #56: DANGLING INTRODUCTORY INFINITIVES

Like participial phrases, infinitive phrases should refer to the subject of the sentence, which should appear right after the comma.

No: To enlarge their market, retail showrooms were opened in office centers.
WILL THE SHOWROOMS ENLARGE THE MARKETS?
Yes: To enlarge their market, they opened retail showrooms in office centers.

No: To ensure security of the company's confidential data, a hierarchy of passwords is used.
THE HIERARCHY ASSURES SECURITY?
Yes: To ensure security of their confidential data, the company uses a hierarchy of passwords.

No: To revise the row definitions, DROX is entered.
DROX REVISES THE DEFINITIONS?
Yes: To revise the row definitions, (you) enter DROX.

Certain infinitive phrases, through wide use, become "absolute" (that is, nonmodifying) constructions. Such introductions as *to repeat* or *to conclude* need not be linked to the subject.

BUG #57: DANGLING ENDS

When a participle or other verbal appears in the last phrase of the sentence, be sure it is connected grammatically to the noun that precedes it.

> No: Do not service these terminals when smoking or eating.
> Yes: Do not eat or smoke when you service these terminals.

> No: Create a new file to keep the archive data safe.
> Yes: To keep the archive data safe, (you should) create a new file.

Careless attachment of verbal phrases causes sentences that vary from confusing to absurd. Consider this monstrosity:

> No: The patient left the hospital urinating comfortably.
> Yes: When the patient left the hospital, he could urinate comfortably.

BUG #58: INCOMPLETE CONTRASTS

Often, the best way to define something is both to say what it is and say what it is NOT. To explain a feature, an action, benefit, or a method, describe its rejected alternative. Use contrast.

> No: The standard report shows only quarterly and yearly summaries.
> Yes: The standard report shows only quarterly and yearly summaries, not monthly summaries.

> No: We want better trained operators and shorter training programs.
> Yes: We want better trained operators, but we want shorter, not longer, training programs.

> No: These models can be used even by nonfinancial executives.
> Yes: These models can be used not only by financial executives, but even by nonfinancial executives.

The trouble is that many writers, and even many professional editors, object to these insertions as "redundant" verbiage. They point out that the No and Yes versions are logically equivalent; so, they prefer the shorter form.

But that objection misses the point. Writing in government and industry needs not only facts but **emphases**. "Unnecessary" contrasts help the writer do what is so easy for speakers: make the audience notice what is important.

BUG #59: FAULTY PARALLEL—SHORT LIST

The words *and*, *or*, and *nor* cause the reader to expect that what will follow these words is parallel in grammatical form to what preceded them. For example, one or two adjectives before an and *call* for an adjective after the and.

Parallel Adjectives

No: This new printer is faster, quieter, and will break down less often.
Yes: This new printer is faster, quieter, and more reliable.

Parallel Nouns

No: The President thanked them for their loyalty, dedication, and because they worked through
      the power crisis.
Yes: The President thanked them for their loyalty, dedication, and willingness to work through
      the power crisis.

BUG #60: FAULTY PARALLEL—LONG LIST

Items put into long lists—with numbers, letters, or "bullets" to set them off—should nearly always be in parallel. In a first-draft list of four or five items, usually two or three will be in parallel form already; the quickest way to edit is to generalize the form of those already-parallel items to all others in the list.

No: We'll know the new productivity program is working when we see the staff:

· arriving at work on time
· correct their own mistakes
· stay out of accidents
· less absenteeism

Yes: We'll know the new productivity program is working when we see the staff:

· arriving at work on time
· correcting their own mistakes
· staying out of accidents
· using less sick leave

OR

Yes: We'll know the new productivity program is working when we see:

· less lateness
· less absenteeism
· fewer accidents
· fewer mistakes

Interestingly, the only time a good writer will actually strip information from a passage is to make it more nearly parallel, easier to read. Sentences that are not parallel almost always force the reader to restart the sentence or clause in which the problem occurs.

NOTE: Listing items with "bullets" used to be considered too informal for professional writing. Today, however, bullets are **preferred** to letters or numbers. In fact, today's writers use numbers or letters only when they are meaningful—when they represent actual sequence or priority.

BUG #61: FAULTY PARALLEL—COMPOUNDS

Whenever you write a compound subject, compound verb, or compound modifier, be sure all of its components are parallel.

No: We mean to be at the airport by 8 a.m. and arriving at the site by 10.
Yes: We mean to be at the airport by 8 a.m. and to arrive at the site by 10.

No: He had to learn not to switch between following his plan and to bob up and down with every new fad.
Yes: He had to learn not to switch between following his plan and bobbing up and down with every new fad.

No: Our alternatives were to go ahead and cut the purchase order or having more vendors make presentations.
Yes: Our alternatives were to go ahead and cut the purchase order or to have more vendors make presentations.

BUG #62: INVERTED COMPLEX SENTENCES

A complex sentence has a main (or independent) clause and one or more subordinate (or dependent) clauses. Usually, the important information, the "payload," is in the main clause. So, a complex sentence usually reads better with the subordinate clause first.

Be sure that your fear of *because* does not trap you into putting the *because*-clause last when it should be first.

No: We have stopped using the U.S.P.S. because of the delays we described.
Yes: Because of the delays we described, we have stopped using the U.S.P.S.

No: This plan will never satisfy the sponsor, even though the consultants love it.
Yes: Even though the consultants love this plan, it will never satisfy the sponsor.

Should you ever put the subordinate clause last? Of course—if it is the part of the sentence you want to emphasize. Often this is the case when the subordinate clause is a kind of meaningful afterthought, a parting shot:

We accepted the bid, even though it was much higher than the projection.
    OR
We accepted the bid—even though it was much higher than the projection.

BUG #63: *THERE*-SENTENCES

Sentences beginning with *there are* or *there is* are sometimes an effective way to emphasize the phrase that follows. To be effective, though, they must be used sparingly. When they are used habitually, they make our writing stiff and clumsy.

    No: There are seven consoles that feed text into the main processor unit.
    Yes: Seven consoles feed text into the main processor.

    No: There is a reason that we did not bid on the RFP.
    Yes: We had a reason for not bidding on the RFP.

    No: There was available a scanner that could reduce the number of input consoles.
    Yes: A scanner was available that could reduce the number of input consoles.

There-sentences work best at the beginning of a section (for example, "There are four issues..."). If you use them only occasionally, they will help you make your points. Overused, they muddle your ideas.

BUG #64: *IT*-SENTENCES

Sentences beginning with *it is* or *it was* are sometimes an effective way to emphasize the phrase that follows. To be effective, though, they must be used sparingly. When they are used habitually, they make our writing stiff and clumsy.

> No: It is obvious that they cannot afford our product.
> Yes: Obviously, they cannot afford our product.

> No: It is difficult to follow this protocol.
> Yes: Following this protocol is difficult.

> No: It was not our purpose to criticize our competitor's product.
> Yes: We did not intend to criticize our competitor's product.

BUG #65: MARATHON SENTENCES

A marathon sentence is one with 26 words or more. Although some good writers can craft clear, readable sentences with 50 or 100 words, most average writers should stay below 20 words. In manuals, procedures, or instructions, the ideal average is 13–17 words.

Marathon sentences result from two mistakes: using too many words to express simple ideas, and putting too much information in one sentence.

Wordy

No: The general feeling of the meeting was that within the framework of the tests a great deal has been accomplished and learned by all parties, and the prototype system has achieved most of the objectives with regard to showing the functional capabilities of SHIP under an INFO/TSO environment.

Yes: At the meeting everyone agreed that the tests were successful, having proved that SHIP works efficiently under INFO/TSO.

Crowed

No: In addition to solid, dashed, phantom, centerline, and invisible line fonts, numerous linestring fonts are available that provide generation about a centerline with variable spacing (width), layer of insertion options, and left, right, and center justifications.

Yes: The available line fonts are solid, dashed, phantom, centerline, and invisible. There are also linestring fonts that generate about a centerline. These linestring fonts can vary spacing (width), insert layers of information, and justify text to the right, left, or center.

BUG #66: PRIMER SENTENCES

For most readers, strings of very short sentences (fewer than 10 words) seem choppy and distracting. They are acceptable in procedures—especially those to be read and followed in a noisy factory. And they are necessary for readers with poor reading skills or limited education. But, in most scientific and business communication, they seem immature and childlike. Thus, many editors call them "primer" sentences.

Too Simple

The process is very simple. Each file is described in terms of its attributes. Any attribute can be changed. There is a design command for each attribute. To change a file, change one or more attributes.

More Mature

Put simply, each file is defined as a set of attributes, any of which can be changed. Because there is one command uniquely associated with each attribute, you can redefine the file by entering those commands that correspond to the attributes you wish to change.

The habit of writing in tiny, primer sentences prevents some writers from communicating **ideas** that often call for complex sentences.

No: We thought they would be cooler. We did not know that they would also be cheaper.
Yes: They are not only cooler but cheaper.

No: This test procedure is not mentioned in the Scope of Work. However, it exceeds the specifications.
Yes: Although not mentioned in the Scope of Work, this test procedure still exceeds the specifications.

Save short sentences for high-impact statements.

BUG #67: CLAUSES INTO PHRASES

Often, you can improve a sentence by converting a long clause into a shorter phrase.

No: While they were waiting for the report to print, they reviewed the last run.

Yes: During the wait for the report, they reviewed the last run.

    OR

Yes: While waiting for the report to print, they reviewed the last run.

No: Once the meeting had been finished, we were ready to draft the specs.

Yes: After the meeting, we were ready to draft the specs.

    OR

Yes: The meeting over, we were ready to draft the specs.

No: We incorporated the changes that were determined by factors in the economy.

Yes: We incorporated the economically determined changes.

BUG #68: CLAUSES INTO WORDS

Once in a while, you can improve a sentence by converting a whole clause into a single word.

No: Store the data in a file that provides access to all users.
Yes: Store the data in a file accessible to all users.

No: He doubted that the data were what is considered the most timely available.
Yes: He doubted the timeliness of the data.

(WARNING: Resist the temptation to convert all prepositional phrases into modifiers; do not replace *evaluation of the plan* with *plan evaluation*.)

Instead of	Write
As is now apparent to me	Apparently
We now think it likely that	Probably
What all this clarifies is	Clearly
I can now assure you that	Certainly

LINKS

LINK PROBLEMS

Each of the sentences and passages below has trouble with "links"—the small words we use to connect one clause to another or one sentence to another. Look out for

- weak connections
- illogical connections
- places where a connection is needed but absent
- cases where the link is confusing, distracting, or cryptic

69. The Invitation for Bids was sent out very late and we had only three days to prepare an answer.

_____

_____

(Remedy: Page 105)

70. This system is not standalone, but all you need to add is a monitor.

_____

(Remedy: Page105)

71. Structured programming reduces the cost of software engineering. GIGO claims that it spends
    30% less for programmer services.

_____

_____

(Remedy: Page 105)

72. This package makes it much easier to generate our monthly financial reports. However, it will
    make it harder to update our financial files.

_____

(Remedy: Page 105)

73. Top-down programming simplifies the work of the junior programmers and thereby saves time and money. Unfortunately, this makes the programming function less interesting.

_____

_____

(Remedy: Page 105)

LINK REMEDIES

69. Because the Invitation for Bids was sent out so late, we had only three days to prepare an offer.

   See Bug #69: *And* (Page 106)

70. Although this system is not standalone, all you need to add is a monitor.

   See Bug #70: *But* (Page 107)

71. Structured programming reduces the cost of software engineering. For example, GIGO claims that it now spends 30% less for programmer services.

   See Bug #71: Transitional Words (Page 108)

72. This package makes it much easier to generate our monthly financial reports. It will make it harder, however, to update our financial files.

   See Bug #72: *However* (Page 109)

73. Top-down programming simplifies the work of junior programmers and thereby saves time and money. Unfortunately, this simplification makes the programming function less interesting.

   See Bug #73: Cryptic References (Page 110)

BUG #69: *AND*

And is the weakest and most dangerous of all linking words. When two clauses are connected with an *and*, we know nothing more than that they are related—somehow. (*And* means little more than a semicolon.)

Look for more interesting connections. In particular, look for complex sentences. For example

> The system uses 20 commands and most users can learn these in two hours.

What is the connection between these two facts? Here are some possibilities.

- Because the system uses only 20 commands, most users can learn it in just 2 hours.
- Even though the system uses 20 commands, most users can learn them in just 2 hours.
- Not only does the system use 20 commands, but most users can also learn them in just 2 hours.
- The system uses just 20 commands, which, typically, users can learn in only 2 hours.
- Despite its 20 separate commands, the system can be learned in only 2 hours.

BUG #70: *BUT*

The word *but* is trickier than most people think. It is a synonym for *however* and should be used to show that the second statement contradicts, limits, contrasts with, or denies the first statement.

One problem arises when the first statement is negative.

First Statement

He never used a calculator.

Second Statement

He worked lightning fast with a slide rule.

Because these two statements do not contradict each other in any way, it would be a mistake to join them with a *but*.

No: He never used a calculator but was lightning fast with a slide rule.
Yes: Although he never used a calculator, he was lightning fast with a slide rule.

Even when the first sentence (clause) is not negative, be careful of using *but* to connect two statements that are not in any way contradictory. For example

No: The first low-cost calculators were advertised in 1974, but few were sold before 1975.
Yes: Even though the first low-cost calculators were advertised in 1974, few were sold before
       1975.

Even though both "No" examples may sound correct to many writers, in both instances, the idea lends itself best to an *although*-sentence (which may also begin with *even though*, *while* or similar terms). This paradigm is frequently the solution to the problem of misused *but*s and *however*s.

NOTE: There is no rule of grammar that prohibits you from starting a sentence with *but*—as long as that sentence contradicts or limits the previous one.

BUG #71: TRANSITIONAL WORDS

Too often, the sentences in a paragraph are disconnected from each other. The writer knows how they are linked, but the reader cannot see the pattern. When you write, be sure you know the rule or logic that connects each pair of sentences. And use transitional words and phrases to guide the reader. The most useful transitionals are:

To Extend or Elaborate

then
first, second, etc.
finally
in fact, indeed
for example
further, furthermore
moreover
next
soon
in addition, additionally

To Assert Consequence

accordingly
consequently
thus, therefore
in short, in sum
in conclusion, to conclude
as a result
for these reasons
given
then

To Refer

from this
meanwhile
after that
before that
lately, recently
formerly, previously

To Concede

of course
even so
granted
admittedly
still
after all

To Stress Similarities

similarly
likewise
in the same way
just as
at the same time
along these lines
by analogy
comparably
for example
to illustrate

To Highlight

to be sure
indeed
certainly
clearly

To Contrast

yet, still
however, but
nevertheless, nonetheless
on the contrary, in contrast
on the other hand
although, though, albeit

WARNING: Battle any editor who tries to strip away these transitional phrases.

BUG #72: *HOWEVER*

The word *however* is more effective when it appears a few words into the sentence, rather than at the very beginning. (The terms *in contrast*, *on the other hand*, and *though* work similarly.)

Put *however* after the word or phrase that you are contrasting with the previous sentence.

Given: Most writers put *however* at the beginning of a sentence.
No: However, I prefer it later in the sentence.
Yes: I, however, prefer it later in the sentence.

Given: Most database management systems have complicated rules for the structure of the files.
No: However, INFO-III has flexible rules for file structure.
Yes: INFO-III, however, has flexible rules for file structure.

Given: We had planned to run our payroll on the company computer.
No: However, our machine is not large enough to handle the job.
Yes: Our machine is not large enough, however, to handle the job.

Sometimes you will have to recast the second sentence a bit, so that the *however* can appear within the first few words. Strictly speaking, however, you can put *however* anywhere. It seems strange when it is the last word, however.

When you really want to start a sentence with *however*, try *but* instead. Of course, many of your colleagues believe (incorrectly) that there is a rule against starting sentences with conjunctions like *but*. Test the waters first; if the outcry is too loud, back off.

BUG #73: CRYPTIC REFERENCES

Pointer words—*this, that, they, these, those, it, which,* and the like—are essential for linking ideas. Be sure, though, that these pointers point unmistakably at one noun, phrase, or clause. When in doubt, repeat the noun or find some other construction.

> No: Heuristic decision models solve problems for which there are no optimization techniques; these are described in the next chapter.
>
> Yes: Heuristic decision models solve problems for which there are no optimization techniques; these models are described in the next chapter.
>
> OR
>
> Yes: Heuristic decision models (described in the next chapter) solve problems for which there are no optimization techniques.

> No: When you try to sell analysis tools to some managers, you learn that they do not use quantitative management techniques. This makes a problem for the sales reps.
>
> Yes: When you try to sell analysis tools to some managers, you learn that these managers do not use quantitative management techniques. This lack of interest in data is a problem for sales reps.

Do not be afraid to repeat an important word or phrase. Good writers repeat words all the time. Be especially careful of using *it* as a pronoun. Unless the reader is sure what *it* refers to, you would be safer repeating the antecedent.

> No: A database management system permits an executive to generate a report from the finance file, if it has been structured correctly.
>
> Yes: With a database management system, an executive can generate a report from any finance file that has been structured correctly.

GRAMMAR

GRAMMAR PROBLEMS

Most educated adults make relatively few errors of grammar. And the few they make are usually caught and corrected by bosses, editors, typists, or various software proofreaders. Still, errors of grammar, even if they only rarely distort your meaning, can be embarrassing. People who make errors of grammar are often judged as either lazy or stupid.

Below are the few errors of grammar I find most often in the writing of people who should know better. For the sake of this exercise, do not worry so much about whether these sentences are clear or readable. Rather, look for grammatical **mistakes**.

74. A group of Apple enthusiasts are trying to convince the school board to buy their favorite computers for the high school math program.

_____

_____

(Remedy: Page 115)

75. Either the cases of slow service or the high cost of the printer are scaring them away from buying this year.

_____

_____

(Remedy: Page 115)

76. Each of the terminals should be removed from its carrying case before we come to service them.

_____

(Remedy: Page 115)

77. Every operator must complete 80 hours of supervised work before they are allowed to work unsupervised.

_____

_____

(Remedy: Page 115)

78. We need a special keyboard to enter the Greek symbols in these formulae.

_____

(Remedy: Page 115)

79. We need a new criteria for deciding which trade shows to attend.

_____

(Remedy: Page 115)

80. The new steering committee does not consider company-wide benefits, like the original one did.

_____

(Remedy: Page 115)

81. Just because many of our competitors have gone under is no reason for our sales force to be laying down on the job.

_____

_____

(Remedy: Page 115)

82. Any new program which exceeds $50,000 must be approved at corporate headquarters.

_____

(Remedy: Page 115)

GRAMMAR REMEDIES

74. A group of Apple enthusiasts is trying to convince the school board to buy its favorite computers for the high school math program.

   See Bug #74: Agreement—Troublesome Singulars (Page 116)

75. Either the cases of slow service or the high cost of the printer is scaring them away from buying this year.

   See Bug #75: Agreement—Troublesome Compound Subjects (Page 117)

76. Each of the terminals should be removed from its carrying case before we come to service it.

   See Bug #76: Agreement—Nouns and Their Pronouns (Page 118)

77. All operators must complete 80 hours of supervised work before they are allowed to work unsupervised.

   ### OR

   Each operator must complete 80 hours of supervised work before he or she is allowed to work unsupervised.

   See Bug #77: *He* or *She* (Page 119)

78. We need a special keyboard to enter the Greek symbols in these formulas.

   See Bug #78: Irritating Plurals (Page 120)

79. We need a new criterion for deciding which trade shows to attend.

   See Bug #79: Troublesome Plurals (Page 121)

80. The new steering committee does not consider company-wide benefits, as the original one did.

   See Bug #80: *Like/As*   (Page 122)

81. Just because many of our competitors have gone under is no reason for our sales force to be lying down on the job.

   See Bug #81: *Lie/Lay* (Page 123)

82. Any new program that exceeds $50,000 must be approved at corporate headquarters.

   See Bug #82: *Which/That* (Page 124)

BUG #74: AGREEMENT—TROUBLESOME SINGULARS

Everyone knows that singular subjects take singular verbs and that plural subjects take plural verbs.

Often, though, we are misled by some noun that appears between the subject and verb.

> No: Each of the files need purging.
> Yes: Each of the files needs purging.
> > OR
> Yes: All of the files need purging.

> No: The current generation of programmers never use coding sheets.
> Yes: The current generation of programmers never uses coding sheets.
> > OR
> Yes: Today's programmers never use coding sheets.

> No: An estimate of how long it would take to implement the full security requirements are beyond the scope of this report.
> Yes: An estimate of how long it would take to implement the full security requirements is beyond the scope of this report.

> No: A more detailed discussion of how to apply security and what security is available are contained later in this guide.
> Yes: A more detailed discussion of how to apply security and what security is available is contained later in this guide.

Be especially careful of subjects that start with a singular noun, but seem to become plural—*each of the engineers, a group of physicians, the majority of voters.* These subjects generally take singular verbs. (*None* takes the singular when its meaning is *not one;* plural when its meaning is *not any.*)

BUG #75: AGREEMENT—TROUBLESOME COMPOUND SUBJECTS

When the subject of a sentence is in the *either-or* format, be sure that the number of the verb is the same as the number of that part of the subject closest to the verb.

> Yes: Either the new enforcement policy or the stricter security procedures are likely to reduce the theft.
>
> Yes: Either the stricter security procedures or the new enforcement policy is likely to reduce the theft.

Editors disagree about the rule for *neither-nor*. Some want to use the same principle that governs *either-or*, while others argue that the verb in any *neither-nor* sentence should be **singular**.

BUG #76: AGREEMENT—NOUNS AND THEIR PRONOUNS

Singular nouns demand singular pronouns. The treacherous cases are those in which the subject contains *one, none, each, every, everyone*, and *everybody*. These call for the singular pronouns *he, she, he or she,* or *it*, rather than the plural pronoun *they*.

> No: Each of these monitors must be tested before I'll pay for them.
> Yes: Each of these monitors must be tested before I'll pay for it.
>   OR
> Yes: All of these monitors must be tested before I'll pay for them.

> No: The research team completed their study.
> Yes: The research team completed its study.

(NOTE: The possessive of *it* is *its*, NOT *it's*.)

> No: Not one of the programmers remembered their ID.
> Yes: Not one of the programmers remembered his or her ID.

BUG #77: *HIS or HER*

Pronouns should be of the same number as the nouns to which they refer. In no case, however, may the singular *he* (*him, his*) be used to refer to persons of both sexes or persons whose sex is unknown or irrelevant. The tradition of using masculine nouns and pronouns as "generics" for all humans is repugnant to most female readers and a sizable number of male readers as well. Good writers just do not offend or irritate their readers—especially over a problem as easily remedied as this one.

Where once we used *he*, we now write *he or she*, or *him or her*, or *his or her*, as the situation demands. To avoid these somewhat cumbersome expressions, we can also recast the sentence in the plural. But, under no circumstance, should anyone use *their* in the place of *his or her*.

> No: Each user assigns their password protection to the job.
> Yes: Each user assigns his or her password protection to the job.
> > OR
> Yes: All users assign their password protection to their jobs.

> No: Every vendor must submit their bid by Friday at 5 p.m.
> Yes: Every vendor must submit his or her bid by Friday at 5 p.m.
> > OR
> Yes: Every vendor must submit its bid by Friday at 5 p.m.
> > OR
> Yes: Vendors must submit their bids by Friday at 5 p.m.

Be skeptical of slashed words (*his/her*) and made-up pronouns like *s/he*. These neologisms slow or stop the reader; put simply, we don't know how to read them, and so, they distract us from the substance of the text.

BUG #78: IRRITATING PLURALS

Increasingly, modern writers and editors prefer English-style plurals to Latin-style plurals. These Latin plurals are not wrong—just a bit stuffy and archaic. For example

Old-Fashioned	Preferred
honoraria	honorariums
formulae	formulas
stadia	stadiums
appendices	appendixes
addenda	addendums
indices	indexes

There is, of course, considerable disagreement among good writers on the acceptability of these classical plurals. I recommend the more modern form—except when your employer's style guide, or the journal that might publish your paper, prefers the older form. This issue is hardly important enough to debate.

BUG #79: TROUBLESOME PLURALS

Certain plurals, because they are Latin or Greek, tend to confuse modern writers. Be careful of these:

Singular	Plural
phenomenon	phenomena
criterion	criteria
thesis	theses
medium	media

Media is hotly contested. Many educated people use *media* as a singular, meaning "the press." My own view is that, since TV is a medium, and radio is a medium, there is still a reason to preserve the singular/plural distinction. Outside of data processing and biology, the expression *a media* or *different medias* is so bizarre as to call attention to itself and embarrass the speaker or writer.

Although the style guides for most scientific journals consider *data* plural, most corporations—including the largest computer firms—prefer the singular. You may use it as either a singular or plural—provided you use it one way or the other all the time, and use it in a manner consistent with your industry's or profession's standards. (*Datum*, although it is used in modern science and technology, is no longer the singular of *data*.) I recommend that each company or agency have a policy on the word, so that everyone uses it consistently.

BUG #80: *LIKE/AS*

Like is a preposition, not a conjunction. *Like* introduces a prepositional phrase; it is followed shortly by a noun. *Like* must not appear before a noun, however, if the noun is followed by a verb. Also, *like* cannot be used to compare incomparable ideas.

> No: Their hardware was excellent, like their software was.
> Yes: Their hardware was excellent, as was their software.
> > OR
> Yes: Their hardware was excellent, like their software.

> No: Attach the VDT just like you connect a TV set.
> Yes: Attach the VDT as you would connect a TV set.

> No: The system is expandable, like we would expect from its modular design.
> Yes: The system is expandable, as we would expect from its modular design.

> No: Like the car industry, smallness is everything in this year's computers.
> Yes: As in the car industry, smallness is everything in this year's computers.

Like is tricky. But do not be so afraid of it that you never use the word in places where it is appropriate. (HINT: If you can insert the old-fashioned expression "alike unto a" into a certain place in the sentence, and the sentence still makes sense, then *like* is probably acceptable.)

> Yes: Think like a lawyer.
> Yes: This phase is like a filter.
> Yes: Like the car industry, the computer industry is obsessed with size.

BUG #81: *LIE/LAY*

There are three verbs that get hopelessly confused:

- To lie (repose, rest)
- To lay (put, place)
- To lie (tell falsehoods)

Here are the partial conjugations:

To Lie (repose)

Today, I lie (down) on the couch. [present]

Yesterday, I lay (down) on the couch. [past]

I have often lain on the couch. [past participle]

To Lay (put)

Today, I lay my equipment down on the bench. [present]

Yesterday, I laid my equipment down on the bench. [past]

I have often laid my equipment down on the bench. [past participle]

To Lie (tell falsehoods)

Today, I lie to my boss. [present]

Yesterday, I lied to my boss. [past]

I have often lied to my boss. [past participle]

The main grammatical difference between *lie* (repose) and *lay* (put) is that *lay* is transitive and takes an object. You can lay things, but you cannot lie things. Be especially careful in the past tense:

No: The template was laying on the bench.

Yes: The template was lying on the bench.

The best way to avoid this problem is just to memorize the conjugations, including the illustrative sentences above. Using the wrong form of *lie* or *lay* could undermine an otherwise effective presentation or paper.

BUG #82: *WHICH/THAT*

Use *which* for nonrestrictive clauses (clauses that could be put in parentheses or removed entirely) and *that* for restrictive clauses (clauses that cannot be removed without distorting the meaning). Most of us do just that when we speak, but replace *that* with *which* in a misguided attempt to make our writing more formal. Nonrestrictive clauses are set off with commas; be suspicious of a *which* that does not have a comma before it.

> No: We could not locate the part which was missing.
> Yes: We could not locate the part that was missing.

> No: The proposal which we liked best was from Omega Company.
> Yes: The proposal that we liked best was from Omega Company.

NOTE: The sentences below are different in meaning.

> 1. We rejected the last bid, which was sent by fax.
>   (The last bid happens to have been faxed.)

> 2. We rejected the last bid that was sent by fax.
>   (Not necessarily the last bid.)

Understand that some of the best writers working in English do not bother with this distinction and use *which* in both cases. I recommend the use of *that* for restrictive clauses mainly because technical professionals overuse *which* as a connective. If they were more various or imaginative in their sentence patters, there would be fewer *which*es. Because they are not, though, I propose the *which/that* distinction as a way of improving the flow of business and technical writing.

If there is already a *that* nearby, it is **better** to start the restrictive clause with *which:*

> Here is a program which eliminates that cursor problem.

PUNCTUATION

PUNCTUATION PROBLEMS

Sometimes an error of punctuation will have the same effect as an error of grammar: give the impression that the writer is lazy, or even a little stupid.

Most problems of punctuation, though, affect less the clarity of a sentence than the ease with which others can follow your thinking. By using no punctuation, or the wrong punctuation, you increase the burden on your reader. In the sentences below, look for both kinds of problem:

- incorrect punctuation
- useless, inadequate punctuation

83. I am pleased that this plan has been so well-received, however we cannot proceed with the idea.

_____

(Remedy: Page 129)

84. This package, file structures, report generators, and JCL, will solve your monthly report problems.

_____

_____

(Remedy: Page 129)

85. Almost from the first computers did more printing than calculating.

_____

(Remedy: Page 129)

86. The videotape is called "APL for Young Programmers".

_____

(Remedy: Page 129)

87. I agree that some of the conclusions are weak, but I'll never agree that my data are "hearsay!"

_____

_____

(Remedy: Page 129)

88. His analysis—and I don't agree with this—is that we ought to encourage employees to take their terminals home on weekends—a crazy idea if I ever heard one.

_____

_____

(Remedy: Page 129)

89. The programming course was a pre-requisite for the systems analysis course.

_____

_____

(Remedy: Page 130)

90. The most likely market is a growing city without a major university; a city with consulting needs but not many consultants.

_____

_____

(Remedy: Page 130)

91 . Our objections are: (a) not enough successful implementations, and, (b) not enough field service.

_____

_____

(Remedy: Page 130)

PUNCTUATION REMEDIES

83. I am pleased that this plan has been so well-received; we cannot, however, proceed with the idea.

    OR

I am pleased that the plan has been so well-received, but we cannot proceed with the idea.

    OR

Although I am pleased that the plan has been so well-received, we cannot proceed with the idea.

    See Bug #83: Commas—Splices (Page 131)

84. This package—file structures, report generators, and JCL—will solve your monthly report problems.

    See Bug #84: Commas—Double Function (Page 132)

85. Almost from the first, computers did more printing than calculating.

    See Bug #85: Commas—Optional (Page 133)

86. The videotape is called "APL for Young Programmers."

    See Bug #86: Quotation Marks—With Periods and Commas (Page 134)

87. I agree that some of the conclusions are weak, but I'll never agree that my data are "hearsay"!

    See Bug #87: Quotation Marks—With Other Punctuation (Page 135)

88. His analysis, which I don't agree with, is that we ought to encourage employees to take their terminals home on weekends—a crazy idea if I ever heard one.

    See Bug #88: Dashes (Page 136)

89. The programming course was a prerequisite for the systems analysis course.

   See Bug #89: Hyphens (Page 137)

90. The most likely market is a growing city without a major university: a city with consulting needs but not many consultants.

   See Bug #90: Semicolons (Page 138)

91. Our objections are, first, not enough successful implementations, and, second, not enough field service.

   See Bug #91: Colons (Page 139)

BUG #83: COMMAS—SPLICES

Do not connect two independent clauses, or two complete sentences, with a comma. This error is one of the most common in first-draft technical documents.

> No: The technical library was inadequate, it had no journals more recent than 1988.
> Yes: The technical library was inadequate. It had no journals more recent than 1988.
>   OR
> Yes: The technical library was inadequate; it had no journals more recent than 1988.
>   OR
> Yes: The technical library was inadequate, having no journals more recent than 1988.
>   OR
> Yes: Because the library had no journals later than 1988, it was inadequate.

The "No" version might be acceptable in an informal note, but not in business or professional communications. Notice all the alternative forms. Notice especially that two sentences linked improperly with a comma often have the same weakness as two clauses linked with *and;* try to replace such sentences with a single sentence that starts with *because* or *although* or *not only*.

BUG #84: COMMAS—DOUBLE FUNCTION

Commas perform so many functions that sometimes they are used to do two different jobs in the same sentence or clause. When two separate functions are nested inside of each other, the sentence can confuse or mislead. To clarify the logic, use "supercommas"—semicolons or dashes—to replace the outermost set of commas. Here are some common examples:

Geographical Series

No: We did tests in Phoenix, Arizona, Yonkers, New York, and Kansas City, Missouri.
Yes: We did tests in Phoenix, Arizona; Yonkers, New York; and Kansas City, Missouri.

Series (with commas inside the listed items)

No: Our list included: desks, chairs, and lamps, filing cabinets and storage boxes, A42 monitors, G81 printers, and tablets, markers, and projectors for the trainers.
Yes: Our list included: desks, chairs, and lamps; filing cabinets and storage boxes; A42 monitors; G81 printers; and tablets, markers, and projectors for the trainers.

(NOTE: Any difficult series is easier to read in itemized, "bullet" form.)

Apposition

No: The vice presidents, managers with vision, dedication, and strength, sat at the head of the table.
Yes: The vice presidents—managers with vision, dedication, and strength—sat at the head of the table.

BUG #85: COMMAS—OPTIONAL

Today's writers and editors use fewer and fewer commas. In contrast to the writers of earlier centuries, who inserted a comma wherever they wanted a breath or pause, modern writers tend to be austere with commas. They fear that too many commas produce clutter and interrupt the flow.

I recommend a different view. I say be generous with commas, not stingy. When commas are optional, go ahead and use them. The more subtle and difficult the design of a sentence, the more helpful the commas.

For example

After an Introductory Phrase

Commas are optional after a short introductory phrase. In most cases, though, the comma will help the reader.

> No: On the one hand ball bearings are still manufactured locally.
> Yes: On the one hand, ball bearings are still manufactured locally.

Before the Conjunction in a Series

Commas before the *and* or other conjunction in a series have been optional since the 1940s. But, optional or not, they are nearly always helpful to the reader.

> No: We sent copies to the engineering, operations and maintenance managers.
> Yes: We sent copies to the engineering, operations, and maintenance managers.

BUG #86: QUOTATION MARKS—WITH PERIODS AND COMMAS

In the United States and Canada, periods and commas ALWAYS go inside quotation marks, whether or not they logically belong there. (This is not true in Europe.)

From the United States Government Printing Office *Style Manual*:

> 8.144. The comma and the final period will be placed inside the quotation marks.

From *The Canadian Style*, published by The Department of the Secretary of State of Canada:

> Place commas and periods within closing quotation marks, whether or not they were included in the original material.
>
> No: After your "sabbatical", we expect you to work extra hard.
> Yes: After your "sabbatical," we expect you to work extra hard.
>
> No: I have no faith in what he calls his "management design".
> Yes: I have no faith in what he calls his "management design."

Do not resist. Although the rule is illogical, nothing is to be gained by breaking it. Those companies that violate this standard in their own style guides (by requiring that all commas be outside quotation marks, for example) do so at their peril.

BUG #87: QUOTATION MARKS—WITH OTHER PUNCTUATION

Colons and semicolons go OUTSIDE quotation marks.

No: The prize for the best paper went to "Drucker's Influence on Management;" it was the only
       paper submitted.

Yes: The prize for the best paper went to "Drucker's Influence on Management"; it was the only
       paper submitted.

Question marks, exclamation points, and dashes go inside or outside, depending on whether they

belong with the quoted material or with the sentence as a whole.

Yes: His speech was called "Who Benefits from the World Bank?"

Yes: Are you the one who described him as "inexperienced"?

Yes: He actually called us "unregenerate liars"!

Yes: "Yes," he said, "Leibniz & Frege Associates are unregenerate liars!"

BUG #88: DASHES

Do not be afraid of the dash; it signals a pause slightly longer than a comma, or it interrupts the sentence for a purposeful digression or a pointed afterthought.

- Type dashes correctly. Word--word. Two hyphens--no spaces.
  (The fonts in many electronic publishing systems contain a real "em- dash," a line much longer than the hyphen. When you type your document, however, you still use two hyphens.)

- If you want to set off an apposition or an interjection within a sentence, be sure to use a dash at both ends. But no more than one pair of dashes to a sentence!

- In less formal messages (like memos), you may even use a dash to connect two closely related sentences. Use the dash instead of the semicolon—don't be afraid.

Dashes are becoming more acceptable all the time. Once considered the punctuation mark of the uneducated, they have become a useful way to provide breathing space in long or complicated sentences, especially when commas are being used for more than one purpose.

BUG #89: HYPHENS

Do not assume that when you add a prefix to a word you must put a hyphen in it. There are relatively few cases where a hyphen is needed; and it is almost never needed when the prefix is *re-*, *pre-*, *sub-*, or *semi-*.

Use a hyphen when

1. The prefix ends in *a* or *i* and the base word starts with the same letter: *anti-intellectual, ultra-adaptive*.
2. The hyphen is needed to prevent mistaking the word you intend for some other word: *reform v. re-form, remark v. re-mark, refuse v. re-fuse*.
3. The prefix is *self-*: *self-addressed, self-administered* (but not *selfsame* or *selfless*).
4. The word is likely to be mispronounced without the hyphen: *co-op, co-worker*.
5. The base is capitalized: *non-American, pro-Israel, pre-EEC*.
6. The base is a number: *pre-1945; post-1978*.

Remember that there is no hyphen in *prerequisite, redesign, subset, infrastructure,* or *supercharged*. When in doubt, consult a dictionary.

BUG #90: SEMICOLONS

A semicolon is almost equivalent to a period. Grammatically, the semicolon is like a comma-fol-lowed-by-*and*. Its beauty is that it allows nearly a full stop (like a period) while still managing to link two large sentences or clauses (like *and*). The semicolon tells the reader that the just-read thought is still incomplete; it creates anticipation.

Be sure, though, that the statement to the right of the semicolon is a complete sentence.

No: We wanted a senior project manager; that is, one who had installed projects on this scale.
Yes: We wanted a senior project manager, that is, one who had installed projects on this scale.

No: Our company has thirty years' experience in graphics software, we are the oldest in the business.
Yes: Our company has thirty years' experience in graphics software; we are the oldest in the business.

No: The plan lacked three ingredients; money, staffing, and willpower.
Yes: The plan lacked three ingredients: money, staffing, and willpower.

Weak: The specifications were odd, and the short deadline was suspicious.
Stronger: The specifications were odd; the short deadline was suspicious.

BUG #91: COLONS

Use colons to introduce a list or a long example: to introduce an explanation or elaboration of what preceded the colon. Be careful, though. The material to the right of the colon may be either a complete sentence or a fragment. The material on the left, however, should be a self-contained statement or sentence (although many modern editors no longer enforce that rule).

No: We bought: 2 printers, 4 monitors, and a character reader.
Yes: We bought 2 printers, 4 monitors, and a character reader.
        OR
Yes: We bought the following items: 2 printers, 4 monitors, 1 character reader.

No: Omega promised us a decision by Thursday: they later told us it would be the following
        Tuesday.
Yes: Omega promised us a decision by Thursday; they later told us it would be the following
        Tuesday.
        OR
Yes: Omega asked for another extension: to next Tuesday.

Weak: He overlooked the most serious flaw, which was that the table headings were abbreviated.
Stronger: He overlooked the most serious flaw: the abbreviated table headings.

"STYLE"

"STYLE" PROBLEMS

Sometimes, a writer has certain bad habits that appear on nearly every page—or even in every paragraph. The effect of these chronic mistakes is that the writing gets an odd look or sound to it. In extreme cases, the language seems like a variant dialect of English, as though the writer had a language of his or her own.

Sometimes a whole industry suffers from these style bugs. Many computer professionals, for example, are fond of what I call "The Conehead" style. Many scientists suffer from the affliction I call "Dracula." Examine these sentences for peculiarities of style. Look for

- · weird ways of expressing ordinary ideas
  · stilted, artificial expressions
  · strange terminology and tortuous constructions
  · anything that keeps these passages from sounding like plain, readable English

92. Clerical processing personnel should demonstrate a capability of entering 250 linguistic characters per minute, with zero error units, prior to employment selection.

(Remedy: Page 145)

93. It is required that a copy of the completed adjustment form be sent to the manager as soon after the reconciliation of the account as is feasible.

(Remedy: Page 145)

94. Please be advised that we have formulated no opinion pursuant to your interrogatory.

(Remedy: Page 145)

95. Should you decide to expand your system in the future, do not hesitate to call upon us for additional advice and assistance.

_____

(Remedy: Page 145)

96. Please read attached memo from database manager.

_____

(Remedy: Page 145)

97. It was asserted that the performance of this company failed to meet the expectations in the contract.

_____

_____

(Remedy: Page 145)

98. The sponsor, i.e., the Air Force, had some concerns re our past contract, e.g., cost overruns and late progress reports.

_____

(Remedy: Page 145)

99. They will not be able to finalize their decision until they prioritize the site selection criteria.

_____

(Remedy: Page 145)

100. Optimally, we ought to be able to install and test the system in five weeks, maximum.

_____

_____

(Remedy: Page 145)

"STYLE" REMEDIES

92. To be hired, clerks must be able to type 50 words a minute (250 characters) without errors.

    See Bug #92: The Conehead (Page 146)

93. As soon as the account is reconciled, send the manager a completed adjustment form.

    See Bug #93: The Coward (Page 147)

94. We have not yet made up our minds about your request.

    See Bug #94: The Lawyer (Page 148)

95. If you decide later to expand your system, be sure to ask us for advice and help.

    See Bug #95: The Robot (Page 149)

96. Please read the attached memo from the database manager.

    See Bug #96: The Telegrapher (Page 150)

97. They complained that we had not lived up to the contract.

    See Bug #97: Dracula (Page 151)

98. The sponsor, the Air Force, had some concerns about our past contract—mainly our cost overruns and late progress reports.

    See Bug #98: The Ambassador (Page 152)

99. They will not reach a final decision until they rank the site selection criteria.

    See Bug #99: The Ize-Man (Page 153)

100. Ideally, we ought to be able to install and test the system in no more than 5 weeks.

    See Bug #100: The Management Scientist (Page 154)

BUG #92: THE CONEHEAD

The alien Coneheads (from *Saturday Night Live*) have a distinct way of talking. Not only do they refer to ordinary objects by pseudoscientific names (*eggs* become *chicken embryos*), they describe all ordinary processes as though they were items in an instruction manual (*eating* becomes *ingesting consumable nutrients*). Strangely, many people in the computer field write a little like Coneheads.

Conehead English	Earth English
alphabetic characters	letters
application development team	committee
audio monitoring device	speaker
multipurpose financial center	bank
clerical workstation	desk
client base	customers
nonmanufacturing employment unit	office building
personal lifestyle environment	house, home
systems information developer	writer
information dump mindmap	thoughts
instructional facilitator	teacher
negative input	complaint
public mailing facility	post office
print output site	printer
retail shopping facility	store
retail fuel outlet	gas station
surface transport equipment	trucks
voice data communications unit	telephone

BUG #93: THE COWARD

Do not be afraid to give commands. Write in the second person, in the imperative, and tell your reader what to do.

Instead of

1. To find what file names have been assigned, DFIL should be entered.
2. If the user wishes to find what file names have been assigned, he or she should enter DFIL.
3. If one wishes to find what file names have been assigned, one should enter DFIL.
4. The command DFIL can be used to find what file names have been assigned.
5. Users who wish to find what file names have been assigned should enter DFIL.
6. The listing of assigned file names is provided by the command DFIL.
7. In order to see a list of assigned file names, it is necessary that you type DFIL at the command line.
8. Reviewing the list of assigned file names requires the typing of DFIL.

Write

To see what file names have been assigned, type DFIL.

BUG #94: THE LAWYER

Do not use legalistic terms in ordinary business writing—especially at the beginning of your letters.
Please note that the style of writing called "legalese" is as disliked by good lawyers as by anyone else.
Typically, when we try to write "like a lawyer," we end up imitating a mediocre or evasive lawyer.

Instead of

Enclosed please find our response pursuant to your inquiry of Thursday last. We hereby advise
you, as per your request, that we will be sending said refund in due course under separate cover.

Write

We have received and read your letter written last Thursday. We agree that you are entitled to a
refund, which we will send you in just a few days.

If possible, strike the words *enclosed*, *attached*, and *reference* from your letters. Indeed, avoid all
"letter lingo," stuffy and legalistic expressions that you use only in letters and memos. These stale,
hackneyed expressions—for example, "as referenced above"—are so predictable and uninteresting
that they kill the attentiveness of the reader. "Attached please find" becomes "here is."

BUG #95: THE ROBOT

The Robot, who has no real feelings, is fond of tired, inauthentic expressions of courtesy and friendship. It is a style of language we associate with people who are supposed to serve the public but who have come to think of the public as a nuisance. It is also frequently associated with embarrassment: apologizing for delays, breaking bad news, and rejecting applications.

Avoid expressions used regularly by people who are polite or contrite for a living.

Instead of

It has been a pleasure to serve you and we trust that if we can be of additional assistance in the future you will not hesitate to call upon us.

Write

I enjoyed working with you. Call right away if there is anything we can do to help you.
>   OR

I hope we can do business again soon.

Instead of

We regret any inconvenience caused by the delay and trust that you will think of us again when you travel.

Write

[Sorry: Unless you are prepared to compensate people for their inconvenience, the best policy here is to say nothing.]

BUG #96: THE TELEGRAPHER

Some people write as though they were being charged for each word. For some reason, they leave out articles and other function words. Save this style for telegrams—when omitting words is cost-efficient.

> No: When creating new file, ensure new name not assigned to existing file.
> Yes: When you create a new file, be sure its new name has not already been assigned to some other file.

> No: Noted several flaws in process controls. Informed quality assurance engineer of observations.
> Yes: I noticed several flaws in the process controls, and I told the quality assurance engineer what I had seen.

The most telegraphic messages, of course, are "error messages." Because most programmers are reluctant to waste memory on long-winded messages, they write cryptic sentences and fragments that are nearly unintelligible: for example, *invalid number of parameters* or *abort, ignore, fail*, or, worst of all, *Error 157 at Line 1120*.

Given the current low cost of memory, cryptic error messages are no longer justified. Moreover, the cost they exact—frustration, mistakes, downtime, fruitless searches through unreadable manuals—far exceeds the price of the memory saved.

The telegraphic style is acceptable for taking notes, of course, but unacceptable for almost any formal business or technical document.

BUG #97: DRACULA

Dracula sucks the blood and life out of your writing. Although you are trying just to be formal and impersonal, you end up sounding like a zombie.

Write with pronouns. Write about *we*, *you*, and *they*. And write in the active voice of the verb.

Instead of

It was expressed strongly that making the system as simple and easy to use as possible is an integral part of the CALC development. It was accepted that doing this was not a requirement for the initial prototype but that some proof would be necessary before further development could take place.

Write

CALC, they insisted, must be as easy to use as possible. And they warned that unless we could prove the system was going to be simple, they would stop us from going beyond the prototype.

The tradition of avoiding *I* in formal scientific papers does not extend to ordinary business writing. (And there are even many scientists who no longer uphold the prohibition.) Use pronouns and write in the active voice. And use verbs that show feeling and intention.

BUG #98: THE AMBASSADOR

Some writers like to show off their meager knowledge of foreign languages. Unless there is a compelling reason to do otherwise, however, we should all write in English. And when we use foreign expressions, use them correctly. (If you speak them, pronounce them correctly. The *fait* in *fait accompli* rhymes with "bet," not "bait.")

Avoid foreign terms and abbreviations, such as

- a priori
- cause célèbre
- e.g.
- fait accompli
- i.e.
- per (as per)
- qua
- raison d'être
- re (in re)
- via

If you simply must use *e.g.* and *i.e.*, at least use them correctly. Remember that *e.g.* (for example) goes before a list of examples, not *i.e.* (that is).

BUG #99: THE IZE-MAN

The Ize-man, as the name suggests, likes to invent words that end in *-ize* and nouns that end in *-ization*. (Nowadays, quarterbacks are said to "audible-ize.") He (or she) is also fond of many other prefixes and suffixes and likes to make otherwise understandable sentences sound obscure and technical.

Instead of

Our analyzation of the situation is that this organization will need to prioritize its objectives before it can quantize its decision-options and definitize its plans for regionalizing its distributional network.

Write

We think this company should rank its objectives so that it can rate the various choices before it and pick the best arrangement of sites for its distribution centers.

Of course, not all *-ize* words are bad; *cannibalize* and *rhapsodize* are irreplaceable. But a spray of *-ize* and *-ization* endings makes your writing quite dense and uninviting, especially when there are less bizarre words that mean what you wish to say.

BUG #100: THE MANAGEMENT SCIENTIST

A close cousin of the Ize-man is the Management Scientist. His and her favorites are more special-ized, though: *maximum*, *minimum*, *optimum*, and their associated forms.

The terms *maximum*, *minimum*, and *optimum* should be reserved for cases where there is, in fact, a mathematically definable maximum, minimum, or optimum.

> No: This approach will maximize our sales.
> Yes: This approach will increase our sales.
> > OR
> Yes: This approach will maximize our market penetration.

> No: The draft had minimal errors.
> Yes: The draft had very few errors.

> No: Try to optimize this program.
> Yes: Try to reduce the cost to run this program.

> No: What is the optimum approach to the EEC?
> Yes: What is the best approach to the EEC?

Again, restrict these terms to discussions of statistical methods and mathematical constructs.

AFTERWORD

SOFTWARE TOOLS FOR WRITERS

Even if you do not agree with all the specific editorial changes proposed here, you must agree that editing improves sentences. Nearly always, a few minutes spent revising a sentence will make it clearer and easier to read.

Indeed, after many years of consulting with managers and technical professionals, I am satisfied that *caring* and *time* do more to improve a draft than specific tricks of style. A reasonably bright person who really wants to be understood will, given a moment or two to reflect, usually find ways to make sentences better.

Good writers must *care;* they must want to be clear. They must be willing to sacrifice, to endure hard work so that their readers will have an easier time. For those who do not care, the extra time needed to edit, test, and revise seems wasted.

But some very good writers and editors do not get the time they need to make first drafts readable and clear. Many companies, many bosses, still think that clear writing does not matter, that editing is a frill.

Fortunately, though, there are some new computer-based tools to help us with revisions. Not only are there spelling-checkers that catch most of our spelling errors and, more important, nearly all of our typographical errors. Now there are *style-checkers*, inexpensive robots that proofread our drafts and flag certain recurring lapses of grammar and style.

There are programs for every size and type of computer, for every operating system, and every major word processor. They range in price from several hundred dollars to inexpensive "shareware" programs that calculate the Gunning Fog index (a measure of difficulty) and count the number of verbs converted to nouns. To illustrate, consider the following sample:

1 Pursuant to your enquiry of 10 July. Please be advised that

2 we have not yet made a decision regarding our choice of

3 vendor. Each of the vendors has submitted their best and

4 final offer and the group of reviewers are going over all of

5 these documents with the greatest care.

6 Once the offers have been prioritized, the winner will

7 receive a notification. Of course, the possibility of a tie

8 exists. In the event that there is a tie, the two winners

9 will receive an invitation to make a presentation to the

10 committee, in which case each finalist will be judged on the

11 strength of it's presentation and it's ability to answer

12 questions from the commitee.

13 We regret any inconvenience caused by this delay. Please be

14 assured that prior to any presentatation you will be given a

15 sufficient period of time to make your preparations.

This innocent little letter is filled with the bugs we have been discussing, along with some others.

Line 1: "Pursuant to" and "Please be advised" are clichés.

"Enquiry" is misspelled;

"10 July" is military or Canadian.

The first sentence isn't one.

Line 2: "Made a decision regarding" is a smothered verb.

Line 3: The plural "their" is referring to the singular "each."

Line 4: The singular "group" is incorrectly linked to "are."

Line 5: "With the greatest care" is a cliché.

Line 6: "Prioritized" is an unnecessary neologism.

Line 7: "Receive a notification" is a smothered verb. "The possibility. . .exists" is an empty predicate.

Line 8: "In the event that" is prolix for "if."

Line 9: "Receive an invitation" and "make a presentation" are smothered verbs.

Line 10: "In which case. . ." would be better recast as a new sentence.

Line 11: "It's" is used improperly, twice.

Line 12: "Commitee" is misspelled.

Line 13: "We regret. . ." is a cliché.

Line 14: "Prior to" is pompous for "before." "Presentatation" is a typo.

Line 15: "Sufficient" is pompous for "enough." "Make. . .preparations" is a smothered
verb. And "period of time" is unbearable.

To see the power of these style-checking tools, consider the errors that a program called **RightWriter** found in this document:

Exhibit 2: RIGHTWRITER ANALYSIS

Pursuant to your enquiry of 10 July. Please be advised that
^<<* U12. WORDY. REPLACE Pursuant to BY following *>>
<<* G2. IS THIS A COMPLETE SENTENCE? *>>
<<* S14. CONSIDER OMITTING: Please be advised *>>^

we have not yet made a decision regarding our choice of
<<* S5. USE VERB FORM. REPLACE made a decision BY decided *>>
<<* S13. REPLACE regarding BY SIMPLER about or on? *>>

vendor. Each of the vendors has submitted their best and
<<* U9. IS THIS JUSTIFIED? best *>>^

final offer and the group of reviewers are going over all of these documents with the greatest
care.
<<* U9. IS THIS JUSTIFIED? greatest *>>
<<* G3. SPLIT INTO 2 SENTENCES? *>>^
<<* S3. LONG SENTENCE: 27 WORDS *>>^

Once the offers have been prioritized, the winner will
<<* S1. PASSIVE VOICE: been prioritized *>>

receive a notification. Of course, the possibility of a tie
<<* S13. REPLACE possibility BY SIMPLER chance? *>>

exists. In the event that there is a tie, the two winners

       <<* U12. WORDY. REPLACE In the event that BY if *>>

       <<* U12. WORDY. REPLACE that there BY there or that *>>

will receive an invitation to make a presentation to the committee, in which case each finalist will be judged on the

       <<* S1. PASSIVE VOICE: be judged *>>^

strength of it's presentation and it's ability to answer questions from the commitee.

       ^<<* G3. SPLIT INTO 2 SENTENCES? *>>

       ^<<* S3. LONG SENTENCE: 45 WORDS *>>

We regret any inconvenience caused by this delay. Please be

       <<* U21. NEGATIVE: regret any inconvenience *>>

       <<* S11. IS SENTENCE TOO NEGATIVE? *>>^

assured that prior to any presentatation you will be given a

       ^<<* S1. PASSIVE VOICE: be assured *>>

       <<* U12. WORDY. REPLACE prior to BY before *>>

       <<* S1. PASSIVE VOICE: be given *>>^

sufficient period of time to make your preparations.

       ^<<* S13. REPLACE sufficient BY SIMPLER enough? *>>

       <<* U13. REDUNDANT. REPLACE period of time BY period or time *>>

       <<** SUMMARY **>>

READABILITY INDEX: 9.98

      4th   6th   8th   10th   12th   14th

      |****|****|****|****|****|****| | | | |

      SIMPLE |------ GOOD -----| COMPLEX

      Readers need a 10th grade level of education.

STRENGTH INDEX: 0.00

```
0.0            0.5           1.0
|*  |  |  |  |  |  |  |  |  |
WEAK                      STRONG
```

The writing can be made more direct by using:

- the active voice
- shorter sentences
- less wordy phrases
- fewer weak phrases
- more common words

DESCRIPTIVE INDEX: 0.69

```
0.1         0.5        0.9    1.1
|****|****|****|****|****|*** |  |  |  |  |
TERSE | ------------ NORMAL ------------ |  WORDY
```

The use of adjectives and adverbs is normal.

JARGON INDEX: 0.21

<< WORDS TO REVIEW >>

Review this list for negative words (N), jargon (J),
colloquial words (C), misused words (M), misspellings (?),
or words which your reader may not understand (?).

commitee(?) 1	delay(N) 1
enquiry(?) 1	finalist(?) 1
inconvenience(N) 1	not(N) 1
notification(J) 1	presentatation(J) 1
prioritized(?) 1	pursuant(J) 1

regret(N) 1   sufficient(M) 1

winner(?) 1   winners(?) 1

Another popular program, **Grammatik**, catches most of the same problems. In addition, it suggests removing the "of" from "each of the" and "all of these." And it recommends a substitute for "prioritize."

It should be obvious that both of these programs—and others like them—can spot a significant proportion of the errors we make. At the same time, they clearly miss some of the basics (like noun-verb agreement and misuse of "it's").

Both programs also give some irrelevant or misleading advice. **RightWriter** flags every superlative or negative word, and **Grammatik** remarks on every masculine pronoun, unless you instruct them not to.

It is essential that you be able to customize these programs, or at least know when it is safe to ignore them. Style-checkers do best with rules that are mechanical; they do worst with problems of meaning and interpretation.

For example, almost every mature style-checking product flags nearly every passive form of the verb. Given that most adult writers cannot reliably differentiate active from passive verbs, and given all the trouble that passives cause, this feature is worth the price of the whole computer program (if not the cost of the whole computer).

But no style-checker knows when the passive is better, as in a sentence where the passive moves the emphatic material to the end. And, so far, no style-checker offers to rewrite your sentences for you.

Clear writing still needs slow, careful revision. Good writers know that the time spent on editing is, in fact, invested wisely in their careers.

APPENDIXES

APPENDIX A:
A Glossary of Grammar Terms

The terms in this glossary are likely to occur in most discussions of writing, in this book and elsewhere. This list is short and many of its definitions are best understood through pages of examples and illustrations. A serious writer will own a complete "handbook" of English grammar and usage. Appendix B recommends some complete references and authorities.

Active Voice—A form of the verb in which the subject is the agent and acts *through* the verb. This contrasts with the **passive voice**, in which the subject is acted upon.

> <u>Active</u>: The manager authorized the budget.
> <u>Passive</u>: The budget was authorized by the manager.

Adjective—A word that describes (modifies) a noun: *integrated* system, *ingenious* plan, *their* advantage

Adverb—A word that describes (modifies) a verb, an adjective, or another adverb:

> <u>Verb</u>: It compiles *quickly*.
> <u>Adjective</u>: This is an *especially* fast chip.
> <u>Adverb</u>:   She speaks *very* confidently.

Clause—A series of words containing a subject and predicate; a component in a compound or complex sentence.

> <u>Independent</u>: This is the page.
> <u>Dependent</u>: . . . that was missing

Complex Sentence—A sentence with two or more clauses, at least one of which is a dependent (or subordinate) clause.

> <u>Two-Clause</u>: If you build it, he will come.
> <u>Three-Clause</u>: Because items were lost, we replaced the shipment, even though we did not have to.

Compound Sentence—A sentence with two or more independent clauses (but no dependent clauses).

> With *And*: The new model is out and the price is down.
> With *But*: We cannot afford to buy it, but we will rent it for 6 months.

Conjunction—A word used to coordinate words, phrases, or clauses (*and, or, nor, but*) or to subordinate them (*because, if, as, although . . .*).

Dependent Clause—A clause that cannot stand alone as a sentence, but is part of a larger sentence. For example: *If the price is acceptable*, we will buy the system.

Gerund—A verbal used as a noun, typically ending in "-ing": *Testing* saves money.

Independent Clause—A clause that **could** stand alone as a sentence, but is part of a larger sentence. For example: If the price is acceptable, *we will buy the system.*

Infinitive—A verbal that starts with "to" and ends with a verb: We need *to know* soon. There are two ways *to exit.*

Nonrestrictive Clause—A parenthetical clause that can be removed from a sentence without harming the truthfulness or intelligibility of the sentence; it is usually set off with commas (or parentheses). For example: The aiming helmet, *which was developed for fighter pilots*, is now a computer interface.

Noun—A word that names a person, place, concept, or object: *book, wilderness, evolution, Thelonious Monk, positivism. . . .*

Participle—A form of the verb, used with an auxiliary to form certain tenses (*they were running*); a verbal used as an adjective or adjective phrase (*opening number*).

Passive Voice—A form of the verb in which the subject is acted upon:

> The budget *was authorized* by the manager.
> Problems *were predicted.*
> It *was determined* that the charges were correct.

In the active voice these sentences become:

> The manager authorized the budget.
> We predicted problems.
> They determined that the charges were correct.

Phrase—Two or more words that form a unit or entity within a sentence, but not a complete enough one to be a clause or sentence. For example:

> Prepositional Phrase: In the last chapter . . .
> Participial Phrase: Hoping to improve sales . . .

Predicate—The part of a sentence or clause that conveys information about its subject, always containing a verb and sometimes an object or modifier.

> The report *is a revelation*.
> We *bought cables and data switches*.

Preposition—A word used to signal a relationship between a noun (its object) and some other element in the sentence, for example: *after, at, by, down, in, of, past, through* .

Pronoun—A form of the noun said to "take its place." In fact, pronouns are merely a special subset of those nouns:

> Personal: I, you, he, she, it, we, they, mine, yours
> Indicative: This, that, these, those
> Indefinite: Some, any, none, each
> Relative: Who, whose, whom, what, which, that

Restrictive Clause—A clause that is essential to the meaning or truth of a sentence and therefore cannot be removed. For example: We don't want any software *that takes weeks to learn*.

Sentence—Traditionally, a group of words that "expresses a complete thought," typically containing a subject and predicate. In fact, it is very difficult to define what a sentence is; in some ways it is like one of those undefined entities of geometry, clear to those who grasp it but a mystery to those who cannot.

Declarative: The copier is defective.

Interrogative: What is the extension for copier service?

Imperative: (You) Call right away.

Simple Sentence—A sentence containing exactly one clause.

Subject—A word or phrase denoting the actor or agent in a sentence (or that which is acted upon in the passive voice of the verb); that which the sentence talks about or to which it attributes behavior or characteristics.

Active: The *committee* defeated the proposal.

Passive: The *proposal* was defeated by the committee.

APPENDIX B:
Books About Writing

If you are serious about writing better, you will want to *own* a few good books about writing. That is, these books should be on *your* desk (or in *your* computer's memory)—not just in the corporate library or word processing department.

Even if you have your own "spell-checker," you will need your own dictionary. Remember that spell-checkers do not give definitions, and they do not really catch all spelling problems. If you typed "wave" when you really meant "waive," your spell-checker won't help you.

Most of the so-called collegiate dictionaries sold in North America are comparable in depth and usefulness. The one I recommend (and use) is *The American Heritage Dictionary of the English Language* (Houghton Mifflin, latest edition). Its practice of putting the most modern definitions first makes it a more efficient tool than other dictionaries, and the quality of its "usage notes" for controversial words is uniformly high.

Each company or agency needs its own style guide, or, alternately, it can adopt someone else's. Government agencies and firms that do business with the government should get the latest edition of the *Government Printing Office Style Manual* (U.S. Superintendent of Documents, Government Printing Office). In the private sector, the de facto standard seems to be the latest edition of *The Chicago Manual of Style* (University of Chicago Press).

Along with the dictionary and style guide, you will also want a handbook or directory of rules and recurring problems of usage. Although almost any good freshman composition text will do, I recommend the latest edition of *The Gregg Reference Manual,* edited by William Sabin (McGraw-Hill).

There are scores of useful books on technical writing, some of them aimed at particular professions. Among the most useful are

> Day, Robert A. *How to Write and Publish a Scientific Paper, 3rd Edition.* Oryx Press, 1988.
> Pakin, Sandra. *Documentation Development Methodology.* Prentice-Hall, 1982.
> Tichy, H.J. *Effective Writing for Engineers, Managers, Scientists, 2nd Edition.* Wiley, 1988.
> Weiss, Edmond. *The Writing System for Engineers and Scientists.* Prentice-Hall, 1982.

For advanced or professional writers, I strongly recommend

> Barzun, Jacques. *Simple & Direct.* Harper & Row, 1976.
> Williams, Joseph. *Style: Ten Lessons in Clarity & Grace, 2nd Edition.* Scott, Foresman, 1985.
> Zinsser, William. *On Writing Well, 3rd Edition.* Harper & Row, 1985.

Of course, in the 90s and beyond, nearly everyone will be writing on a computer. Not surprisingly, then, many of the references that used to be in book form are available as computer programs that can be stored in memory and activated with a key or two. With enough memory, you can keep a full dictionary and thesaurus on line. (People with CD-ROM drives can even acquire the entire unabridged Oxford English Dictionary as a "hypertext" product, that is, a library of information that can be searched by doing nothing more than "clicking the mouse" on key words and phrases.)

My own computer has online the *Associated Press Stylebook* and the *Complete Secretary's Handbook* (Digital Learning Systems); the latter, despite its title, is filled with information useful to technical professionals, who usually know nearly nothing about the correct way to write and manage business correspondence.

Again, you should own a few of these books. Or others like them. Merely seeing them near your desk (or on your computer's directory) will remind you of the importance of editing.

INDEX

EDMOND H. WEISS is an independent consultant and lecturer on technical writing, management communication, and documentation. He is the author of *The Writing System for Engineers and Scientists* and *How to Write A Usable User Manual*. The latter book, which has been translated into Japanese, is among the most frequently cited and discussed works on user documentation. (An expanded second edition, *How to Write Usable User Documentation,* will be published in 1991 by Oryx Press.)

Usually, WEISS is traveling North America teaching seminars. At other times, though, he lives in Cherry Hill, New Jersey, with his actress wife and two writerly children.